# Home force

Building a connected, engaged
home-based team

# Home
# force

## JO ALILOVIC

**Homeforce:** *A team of passionate and highly skilled workers collaborating from their homes (or other locations) so they can enjoy the lifestyle they want while achieving outstanding business results for their employer.*

First published in 2021 by Joanne Alilovic

A catalogue entry for this book is available from the National Library of Australia.

ISBN: 978-1-922391-99-5

Printed in Australia by McPherson's Printing
Project management and text design by Publish Central
Cover design by Peter Reardon

The paper this book is printed on is certified as environmentally friendly.

**Disclaimer**
The material in this publication is of the nature of general comment only, and does
not represent professional advice. It is not intended to provide specific guidance for
particular circumstances and it should not be relied on as the basis for any decision
to take action or not take action on any matter which it covers. Readers should
obtain professional advice where appropriate, before making any such decision. To the
maximum extent permitted by law, the author and publisher disclaim all responsibility
and liability to any person, arising directly or indirectly from any person taking or not
taking action based on the information in this publication.

'At a time when the traditional workplace is replaced by a flexible, hybrid work environment, *Homeforce* sets out key steps for leaders attempting to negotiate the new normal. It's a must read.'
**Andrew Barnes, founder of The Four Day Week Global Campaign**

'The future of work has arrived, it's more fluid and uncertain than anyone could have predicted; work and home life is now blended without boundaries. *Homeforce* shines a light on our new working reality and how we can embrace the brave new world of remote working by providing a framework for virtual teamwork, taking flexible work as we know it, to a whole new level. Thank you, Jo.'
**Emma Walsh, CEO Parents at Work**

'Joanne did a flexible work education session with our senior Perth and Melbourne leaders and she asked the "why not". She understands the challenges and knows how to make flexible work appeal to your decision makers.'
**Elizabeth Nunez, National People & Culture Director at RSM**

'They said it would never happen but the pandemic made remote working a reality and now it looks like it's here to stay. But it needs careful planning as Jo Alilovic points out in *Homeforce*, a handbook setting out practical steps from someone who knows how to make it really work.

'Many Australians have now experienced the pros and cons of remote working but there's been little professional advice for managers and business owners on how to run your "homeforce". Alilovic fills the gap with this look at practical steps and advice for dealing with the financial, behavioural and legal impact of a new era where working virtually is business as usual.'
**Catherine Fox, Women and work expert, author and journalist**

'Jo has done the homework for you. Pulling on her experience and the evidence, she gives a realistic and practical resource for you to use today. Looking at flexibility from different perspectives, Jo undertakes a comprehensive investigation into *how* to make flexible working really work. Whether you've been thrown into your first management role or have experience and are trying to figure out how to manage staff from afar, Jo has given us all an important tool. This book is everything I love about Jo: informed, accurate and practical.'
**Conrad Liveris, economist and non-profit executive**

'Thanks to the masterclass on flexible working at scale in 2020 due to C-19, Jo gives employers a useful framework to lock in the gains that working from home delivers for business and for your people, inclusive of women.'
**Tania Cecconi CEO, CEOs for Gender Equity Inc**

'I wish this book had been written a decade ago, when my co-founder and I unknowingly started to build out our software company with a 'Homeforce'. We might have been spared a lot of the second-guessing and some of our early challenges. This book is an absolute must for any business looking to *stay in business* in the future. In my opinion, there's no question about the future of work changing. Jo Alilovic's book is powerfully convincing and offers a practical framework to apply to your business starting today.'
**Nicole Baldinu, co-founder and COO WebinarNinja**

'This is a book of its time and for its time. Jo has established herself as a true thought leader in the SME market in recent years, and this book shows that her trailblazing path is nowhere near complete. I've no doubt her writing will inspire and assist businesses of all stripes!'
**Jerome Doraisamy, author of *The Wellness Doctrines* and *Deputy Editor of Lawyers Weekly***

'If ever there was a timely book – this is it. As author Jo Alilovic says – "we're in the midst of the greatest work from home experiment ever". *Homeforce* is smart, practical and deeply inspiring. Jo provides great structure for the reader to help with the establishment of a remote team, but I like that her focus is on treating people as people, not just resources, or little boxes on the screen during a ZOOM call. This is a book that needs to find its way into the hands of entrepreneurs, CEOs, managers and leaders everywhere.'

**Andrew Griffiths, international bestselling author, entrepreneurial futurist and global speaker**

'I'm excited to read this timely guide to navigating the new world of work. Jo Alilovic brings to these pages her sharp legal mind and years of experience advising in the employment law arena. More than that, though, she brings a deep appreciation of what our 21st Century community is actually seeking from work in terms of recognition for a valuable contribution, no matter how, when or where it is made; and a sense of camaraderie and inclusion whether working within or beyond the corporate office. The rules about how we once forged our professional identities through work have been scattered to the four winds. I have a feeling *Homeforce* may be the manifesto we've been waiting for.'

**Ann-Maree David, Executive Director, Queensland, College of Law**

'Working in a global professional services firm in the middle of a worldwide pandemic, I've come to realise we really have no flexible home-based working rule book! When it comes to *successful* flexible home-based working (and I put the emphasis on successful), there are loads of individuals who post their thoughts here and there, but Jo Alilovic is one of the few people I know who speaks from true experience. Having juggled her family, her law career, a fantastic podcast and her successful HR/Legal business – which comprises a flexible, mostly home-based team – Jo understands what works practically, and what doesn't work. I'd follow the advice in her book *Homeforce* any day.'

**Luke Mitchell, Director Consulting, PWC**

'*Homeforce* is the practical guide you've been looking for to help you build the Homeforce your business needs to excel. Jo generously shares a step-by-step framework to help you equip your team with the skills they need to manage a remote team. You can leave the HR and management homework to Jo so you can instead focus on running your business!'

**Lucy Dickens, author, podcast host, speaker, lawyer and legal innovator in law firm transformation**

'In *Homeforce*, Jo Alilovic goes beyond the usual office vs home rhetoric, to address the critical issues involved in creating home-based teams. She uses research, evidence, and her own primary investigations to provide fresh insights and practical guidance. Her work is comprehensive and detailed, yet accessible. Anyone with responsibility for a workforce would do well to read this book. Those establishing, improving, or leading a "homeforce" team should make it a priority.'

**Katherine Thomas, CEO Free Range Lawyers**

'Welcome to your Homeforce! Jo demonstrates that work from home is not a passing fad or a temporary necessity caused by COVID. It is here to stay.

'In *Homeforce*, Jo uses her employment law background and experience in heading up a remote team at 3D HR Legal to create a roadmap you can follow to build and bed down a distributed team. It's a true reflection of the Jo I know, who goes beyond the legal issues to help employers focus on team building and connection alongside the legal elements.'

**Emma Heuston, Founder/Director The Remote Expert**

'Without question COVID-19 has accelerated the work from home movement exponentially, with millions of workers globally transitioning to a home-based working environment overnight. The productivity business case for remote working is very compelling – including reduced interruptions and disruptions that come with open plan working environments, meetings running to time and being on point, and the time and cost saved in not having to commute. Add to this more time with family, regular exercise and more time to rest, and it's not hard to see why working from home, at least some of the time, is so compelling. With COVID we have been offered the opportunity to work differently, and to think differently about how and where we want to work in the future. But will the experiment last beyond the pandemic? Absolutely it will – and Joanne Alilovic's *Homeforce* provides the roadmap we need to make it happen.'

**Kate Christie, productivity specialist, best-selling author, and CEO Time Stylers**

# Contents

# The greatest work from home experiment ever

'Whether you think you can or you think you can't, you're right.'
Henry Ford

Do you remember what it felt like? That moment when COVID-19 became more than something you watched on the news? When it was officially classified as a pandemic and started to show up in your own neighbourhood? All of a sudden, the shelves were empty of things. I'm not talking about the hand sanitiser and toilet paper. No. I'm talking about the keyboards, computer screens and webcams. Desks and office chairs. All the things you need to establish a home office.

It's been said repeatedly that the coronavirus pandemic brought about more change in the way we work than we've seen in the last 100 years. It's the greatest 'work from home experiment' ever. Up until that point in early 2020, flexible working options like working from home were reserved for the privileged few: mostly working mothers, senior executives or owners of businesses who could do as they liked.

The pandemic changed that. We couldn't leave our homes. We couldn't travel using public transport. We couldn't have more than two people in a lift at a time. All of these things meant that if business was to continue, people needed to work from home. Suddenly, everybody was doing it. All the previous excuses for not doing it went out the window. Remote work was now a business essential, not a privilege for the trusted few.

The pandemic, although horrible, has shown the business world and individuals what is possible. It sped up the evolution of work. It's shown us we don't need to be constrained by the limitations of buildings. For many, the only limitation now is how far the internet will reach.

Businesses saw reduced outgoing costs like electricity, taxis and meals. Big business has come out with big statements about workforce changes. Deloitte announced that it would be closing four of its UK offices. Microsoft said in a new remote work policy that it would 'offer as much flexibility as possible'.

People stopped commuting and had more time to spend in other ways – perhaps with their kids, exercising or enjoying their hobbies. People saw what it was like to work in a way that wasn't based on the old industrial concept of going to the factory, churning out the widget and coming home.

They got their life back. And many people preferred this new way of working.

## DON'T LET IT SLIP

But as vaccination rates increase and life returns to 'normal' for some, it will be very easy to slip back into the old way of doing things. Yet various surveys have shown that many people want to keep working remotely – at least some of the time. If you don't provide the opportunity as a business owner or manager, there is a great risk those people will go elsewhere, to a business that offers the flexibility they seek. We all need to act now if we want to entrench effective remote working for the long term. To create and build a business with a Homeforce where the business saves money, employees are happier and productivity is increased. *Win, win.*

The changes made in response to the coronavirus pandemic were very reactionary. We rushed to make changes to ensure business continuity, without thought for the long term. You need to remember that what got you and your team through this period won't serve you well over time. An 'office' on the kitchen table or the ironing board (for those who prefer a stand-up desk) isn't a viable ongoing option. Changes were made to deal with what we all hoped was a short-term crisis, not the future of doing business.

Long-term success with distributed teams requires a lot more planning and attention. In this book, I'll show you how.

## IT'S NOT FOR EVERYONE

Of course, there are some businesses and people who are itching to get back to 'normal', with everybody in one location. That's understandable. Maybe they had a horrid work from home experience filled with fear over their job, worries about getting sick, and the stress of home schooling and sharing the home office with their partner. Combine that with social isolation and it's not surprising some people want 'normal'. Those people want the work from home experiment to end as quickly as possible.

Some owners and managers like being able to see their staff in the office. Some employees like being out of the active wear and back in their fashionable outfits, socialising face to face and escaping their homelife chaos. But this doesn't have to be you. As a business owner or manager, if you and your team have seen the many benefits of life with a Homeforce then you can use this recent crisis as a springboard to a new way of doing business for the future. There is so much potential in a carefully constructed distributed team.

I'm not saying that a Homeforce is for everyone. In fact – there are some jobs and some people who are truly *not* suited to working from home. The people who work in manufacturing jobs, for example. Or who are digging gold out of mines. Or pilots. It isn't possible to do those jobs from home – yet, anyway. But just because some of the jobs in your company can't be done from home doesn't mean you can't have *any* of the jobs done from home. Even if you are in manufacturing, mining or travel, there are going to be some jobs which are office based.

Your Homeforce doesn't have to be your whole workforce. 'Hybrid' is definitely going to be a big buzzword in the 2020s as companies look to combine a central office with a team who like to work remotely. The shift has already happened, and it is definitely going to stay for many people and businesses. It's just a question of whether your business is going to take advantage of the massive opportunity now in front of you.

## THIS FRAMEWORK IS FOR THE FUTURE OF WORK, NOT THE PANDEMIC OF NOW

Unfortunately, as I write this in mid 2021 the pandemic is not over. Businesses and workers everywhere are having to deal with modified forms of operation to meet health and government guidelines and directives.

This book is not going to answer questions like:

- How do I keep my office open during the pandemic?
- Can I require my employees to have the vaccine?
- Can I change my employees' contract of employment because we are experiencing lower demands for work?

It is important to have answers to these questions as we could be dealing with such challenges for years to come. However, you won't find them here. If you want answers to these questions then check out the amazing resources provided by Safe Work Australia and the Fair Work Commission, articles and videos on my website (3dhrlegal.com.au) or get in touch with me directly.

What this book will do is give you a roadmap for creating and embedding a distributed team which will help see your business through the pandemic and beyond.

## THE FRAMEWORK FOR A SUCCESSFUL DISTRIBUTED WORKFORCE

There are six essential steps to building a successful distributed workforce:

1. It all starts with a great vision. You need to know *why you are doing this*. Maybe it's about saving money, about how you engage with your employees or clients, or about how you want to live your own life. Whatever it is, will form the foundation for everything you do after.

2. Next comes analysing your existing business structure – all of the jobs, how people interact with each other and with clients.

3. Third is creating the model terms to ensure workers are safe and productive, that they have the right tools and resources, and that your business is protected.

4. The fourth step is to make sure you have the right people working remotely. It doesn't suit everyone.

5. Next – have an employee focus to ensure solid onboarding and engagement is maintained throughout employment. And put the managers up front and give them the support they need to be fabulous supervisors.

6. Finally, like all good systems, we need to evaluate the whole thing to make sure that we are measuring impact and success. You need to make sure your Homeforce is giving you and your people what you want.

These six steps form the basis of my REMOTE Framework, which we are going to look at throughout this book.

## THE HOW AND THE WHO

I've used my personal business experience running a remote team, as well as my 20 years working as an employment lawyer, to help hundreds of other business owners and managers guide their teams through changes such as embedding flexible work styles, or starting a flexible team from scratch.

Before I walk you through the six-step framework I've created to share this experience and guidance with you, I'm going to set the scene in Part I. I'll walk you through a short history lesson of workplace changes, talk about the benefits of distributed teams, explore the reasons why a Homeforce may not be a good fit for everyone, and then discuss the challenges of transitioning to a distributed team.

Because there *are* challenges – and there will be for you too. To create your own Homeforce for the long term you need to understand all of the benefits *and* the challenges. Only then, once you have considered them and weighed them up in favour of a Homeforce, and made a commitment to it, can you start the steps to make it a long-term reality.

Your Homeforce could be made up of contractors or employees. Talking about the differences between contractors and employees is a whole book unto itself. However, the key points to note for this book are that business owners naturally have more control over the work being done by an employee, and when and where they do it. When you contract work to another business (whether they are a sole trader or not), you are often giving up the right to control the manner of how the work is done. Generally, you are paying that person for an outcome and how they get there isn't your concern.

This book is designed to support businesses with employees working remotely. If you have contractors, you will definitely still get some tips on things to watch out for but your ability to implement may be more limited.

### It works for me – it can work for you

My business has been based around a Homeforce from day one. To start, it was just me, and then over time I added people to the team. All of us work from home. It works very well for us. We get to do work we love, save time on commuting to spend with our families and friends, and we still feel connected with our common purpose to serve our clients well and live a flexible life.

Creating a Homeforce has allowed me to be the business owner I want to be, while being the wife, mother, daughter, sister and friend I also want to be. Too often a business is all consuming, not just for the business owner but also for the people working within it. Having a Homeforce can create more space in your life to have not just a successful business and working experience, but also a more fulfilling life.

### PLANNING YOUR HOMEFORCE

When reading this book I recommend that you have a notebook with you. I'll be asking a lot of questions as we go. It is best if you can pause and consider them and make some notes as you go along. Capture your ideas, start making your plan. You might have some pages for different things. Questions to ask. Experts to find. Business information to obtain.

Read the book with a view to action rather than a view to entertainment. Having said that – I promise lots of funny and interesting anecdotes as I share my own personal stories, those of my clients, and the stories from the business owners I've interviewed and surveyed for this book.

## MAKE THE COMMITMENT NOW

A successful distributed team starts with a commitment now. A commitment to a new way of working.

Having a Homeforce has made a world of difference to me and many of my clients. It started with a commitment to a new way of working. Make that same commitment to yourself and your people now, and I know that following the steps in this book will help you create a Homeforce that makes a difference for you and your team.

PART I

# The changing
# modern workforce

# CHAPTER 1

# Setting the scene

'Productivity is purpose and process, not place. It's driven by why and how we work – not where we work . . . Flexibility is here to stay. Those who reject it may not be.'

Adam Grant

## WHERE DID IT ALL START?

Working from home is not new. Many business owners and employees have been doing this to some extent since the beginning of work. Taking a bit of work home in the briefcase overnight. Catching up on a weekend.

But when did it all become the norm?

Not surprisingly, it really kicked off with the increasing use of technology. We finally got a good moniker for it in the early 1970s when Jack Nilles coined the terms 'telework' and 'telecommuting'. As the years passed the concept gained more and more acceptance, and in the '90s we got the great motto – 'Work is something you do, not something you travel to' – from Woody Leonhard. My favourite variation of this is, 'Work is something we DO, not a place that we GO'.

As the world has opened up and more businesses are operating in a global economy, teams sharing the same space is no longer the only norm. Today, anything goes: working from your car on the road, on planes, trains or buses, in hotel rooms and coffee shops, or at client sites, multiple employer sites and co-working sites – employees have become increasingly adept at working wherever they are with the assistance of technology. Including from home.

The big questions that are coming up now are:

- Do you still need a central office where people go when not with a client or travelling?
- Is it productive to work from home all the time – not just when you need to finish something overnight or on a weekend?

We are already seeing many companies make the choice not to have a central office – or any office at all. GitLab and Automattic are big tech companies that started without an office and now have over 1000 employees working around the globe. And it's not just tech companies. My own small business and others I know are in the same boat without a central office. More and more are looking at it as a real alternative for the future.

## COMMON TERMINOLOGY

After 'telework' and 'telecommuting' a variety of different variations followed, including:

- remote working
- remote first
- fully remote
- working from home (also known as WFH)
- flexible workplace
- distributed workplace
- mobile work
- the virtual office.

The most commonly used terms are 'remote work' and 'working from home'.

Unfortunately, 'working from home' has developed a bit of a negative connotation over time. It is often linked with working mothers, who are sometimes seen as not invested in the workforce. Or we share an understanding smile when asking where someone is and being told they are 'working from home'. As if everyone knows it is code for the fact that the person is slacking off. The other challenge with this expression is that it implies all the work is being done 'at home', and that is not always the case with a person based outside of a central office.

This last issue is catered for by using the alternative expression 'remote work'. This doesn't have as many negative connotations. However, the word itself gives the implication that the person is 'remote' from something or someone. You are distant and away from the main place of action. It gives the impression that there is still a central place, like a central office building. For some businesses, this might still be the case if they continue to maintain a substantial office presence and have a hybrid workforce. For others who lose the office altogether or reduce reliance on it, it just doesn't fit.

These negative connotations and the lack of fit is why I prefer the term 'distributed team'. This expression really is the closest to being exactly what we are creating, whether we have a central office or not. What you are creating is a team with individuals distributed in many different locations, not necessarily all at home, and not 'remote'. They are an active and important part of the whole.

So while I slip back and forth here and there throughout this book, you will mostly see me using the expression 'distributed team'.

## OTHER TYPES OF FLEXIBILITY

Working from home (or anywhere other than a central office) is not the only big change in the world of work in the last 100 years.

It's just one of the flexible work practices which has opened up as we've moved through the industrial and manufacturing eras where we all clocked on and off in the factory, to the knowledge era where we moved into offices and cubicles.

It's important when reading this book not to forget that distributed teams are only one flexible option. Flexible work is about not just where you work, but how and when. We now have many flexible options, including:

- part time
- job sharing
- different start and finish times worked around core hours
- compressed working weeks
- extended leave agreements
- annual fixed duration of remote work.

Many of these things have come about as the workplace has adapted to changes in the labour market. For example, as more women have joined the workforce we have seen an increased uptake in part-time arrangements and the introduction of maternity leave in many countries. It wasn't too long ago my mum was forced to quit her teaching work when she got married. Fortunately, in Australia at least, those days are over. We've also seen the rise in casualisation and the gig economy.

Other ideas seem to have come about because of the pandemic. For example, the idea of a 'workcation', being a block of time where a person can work remotely from anywhere while they are also on holiday. A change of scenery is a great way to improve wellbeing, which means your employee gets a holiday and you get a much more refreshed and productive employee.[1]

All of these types of flexible arrangements can still be implemented when you have a distributed team, so keep them in mind as

---

1   www.cnbc.com/2021/05/10/annual-workcation-tips-for-asking-for-a-month-of-remote-work.html.

you read through this book. Or maybe some of these options can be used where on-site working is required.

## THE HOMEFORCE JOURNEY

As that little history lesson shows, working from home and flexible working arrangements more broadly have been around for a long time. That means many of you may be part way on the journey to a Homeforce already. There are five different stages, as shown in the triangle diagram below.[2]

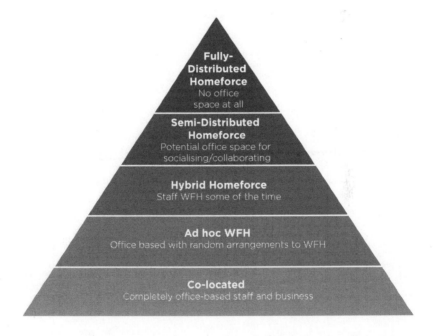

The starting point in the journey (the bottom of the triangle) is where you have a completely office-based business and have never

---

2 Created with inspiration from Matt Mullenweg - 'Distributed Work's Five Levels of Autonomy', (ma.tt/2020/04/five-levels-of-autonomy/).

approved a working from home or remote arrangement. If this is you then you have the longest journey ahead of you.

The next step on the journey is what I call 'Ad hoc WFH', where you have a completely office-based business, however every now and then you have agreed to someone working remotely for a day. Perhaps they needed to be home to wait for a furniture delivery or let the repair person in to fix the water heater. Or perhaps there was a bus strike and it was going to be a nightmare to commute to work that day. Or they needed to be in hospital with an ill child. Whatever the reason, at this point on the journey you've dabbled with remote arrangements but it is still very much office first.

The third stage in the journey is where you have some permanent remote arrangements. These are generally set up so that a portion of the hours of work are done from home, but a fixed percentage are still performed in the office. You've created a Hybrid Homeforce. This often looks exactly like the usual workplace. The same time requirements, same processes and procedures, the only difference is some employees are working from home some (possibly even all) of the time.

For those of you in these middle two stages, you may find the journey the hardest. You might think it will be easier. Why harder, you ask? Because this bit of dabbling may have reinforced misconceived ideas that working remotely is not a full-time option for the majority. It might have thrown up some of the challenges we are going to discuss in detail, like concerns around supervision and productivity. You might have unintentionally reinforced this by not properly setting these employees up to work from home with the right technology, and the right communication protocols with their team. In other words, setting it all up to fail – or at the very least, to not work too well.

The next step is the Semi-Distributed Homeforce: a business with a completely distributed team and no one working routinely in a central office. In other words, employees can work from wherever they like. In this level, the business still maintains a central office that is set up with meeting rooms for team collaboration meetings or meetings with clients.

The top of the triangle, where my business sits, is the Fully-Distributed Homeforce. Not only can your team work from wherever they want, there is also no centrally maintained office. This doesn't mean team members won't come together physically some-times, but it is far from the norm.

You may also have made changes around not just the place of work, but the other key factor of distributed work: when work is to be performed.[3] Rather than everyone still needing to work the usual nine to five you may allow employees the autonomy to work whenever they choose so long as they meet their performance targets. This is a much trickier concept (for reasons we will touch on later), however it is the ultimate in autonomy for employees, and hence what some consider to be the nirvana in distributed work arrangements.[4]

Of course, there are all sorts of stages and versions in between each of these main five levels in the Homeforce journey. Where you ultimately fit and decide to stay will depend on your personal beliefs, the kind of business that you run and your level of commit-ment to change.

If you are already at the top of the pyramid (or the place on the journey you want to be), you're probably wondering why you are reading this book. It's the rare thing that can't do with some improvement. Perhaps you set up your Homeforce in a rush and are now keen to set in place some extra strategies to make it a continued

---

3  'How to do Hybrid Right', Lynda Gratton, *Harvard Business Review* magazine, (May–June 2021) (hbr.org/2021/05/how-to-do-hybrid-right?utm_medium=email&utm_source=newsletter_ weekly&utm_campaign=insider_activesubs&utm_content=signinnudge&deliveryName= DM129267&registration=success).

4  'Distributed Work's Five Levels of Autonomy', Matt Mullenweg (ma.tt/2020/04/ five-levels-of-autonomy/).

success into the future. Perhaps you just want to pat yourself on the back and know that everything is a-ok. Whatever the reason, I'm sure you will still gain something from reading on.

## Why do you want it?

Where do you sit on the spectrum of feeling among business owners about teams working from home? You might be gung-ho in favour of your team being distributed, a fan of it in certain circumstances, or perhaps still sitting on the fence. Maybe you would rather visit the dentist but feel you have no choice but to keep up with workforce changes and be prepared to make the best of it.

\* \* \*

As you can see, I haven't mentioned the business owners and managers who were 'forced' to implement work from home arrangements during the coronavirus pandemic and couldn't wait to get back to the office and back to 'normal'. Those people probably shuddered reading the title of this book, had some unkind thoughts about deluded businesses and quickly walked past.

Wherever you sit, it's worthwhile taking some time here upfront to remind yourself of why it's a good idea to have a distributed team. Whether that is all of them being remote all the time, or some of them some of the time, or any other combo that works for you.

The good reasons are many and aren't just all in the favour of the employee. Don't get me wrong, I'm not saying employees don't win. There are some obvious benefits for employees, like being able to avoid the commute and save time for personal interests, but the advantages for businesses are also great, with a real impact on the bottom line.

## ADVANTAGES FOR EMPLOYEES

The obvious benefit for employees is a massive time saving. No more sitting in the car, bus, train or their other preferred method of transportation. Let's not forget the time spent waiting for public transport. The commute becomes a thing of the past. Instead they can simply get up and walk into their home office. Preferably after at least having a shower and getting out of their PJs. Although – does that really even matter?

Research conducted in 2019 found that not having to commute saves the average Australian worker two hours per day – a whole 10 hours per week.[5] Imagine all the things an employee can do with that time. Exercise for 30 minutes (instead of sitting on a train), prepare a proper home-cooked breakfast (instead of grabbing a toasted sandwich at the office café), take their kids to school (instead of waving them goodbye with the friendly neighbour).

Whenever we get to do more of the things that we want to do, and which make us happy, a bit more work/life balance if you like that expression, we are all around more satisfied and likely to produce better work outcomes. This is a constantly reaffirming cycle. Whenever employees do good work and feel good about it, they are more likely to keep repeating it.

Daniel Pink, author of *Drive*, says the three key things that motivate employees are:

- autonomy
- mastery
- purpose.

---

5   Hopkins, John L, & McKay, Judith (2019) 'Investigating "anywhere working" as a mechanism for alleviating traffic congestion in smart cities.' *Technological Forecasting & Social Change* Vol. 142, May pp258–272 (www.sciencedirect.com/science/article/abs/pii/S0040162518301549?via%3Dihub).

Autonomy can loosely be described as 'choice' – choice in how, where, when and who you work for. Remote work has the potential to give this in spades.

Not just the choice of how you will spend all of your extra time – but bigger choices like where you live. Remote workers can be location independent. Maybe they want to move nearer to elderly relatives to provide care and support. Or to a foreign country to learn a new culture and language. Maybe they just want to live near the beach and swim everyday. Or in the country and go for daily bushwalks. Or maybe they want to be somewhere more exotic like Fiji or South America. (So long as they have a good internet connection, does it matter where they are?)

That's the big picture, but there is a smaller picture too. As Automattic founder Matt Mulleweg said, 'Every employee can have a corner office'. Big offices with kitchenettes and private bathrooms are no longer the benefits of top executives – anyone who works remote can have this, whether in your own home or elsewhere.

Employees also get more choice about who they work for. Employees can potentially work for any company in the world if they are open-minded enough and time zones aren't an issue. If working in an office they are limited by whatever company location they can get to within – God forbid – two hours travel time.

Also – let's not forget the money saving here. Making a guess about some costs – $10 a day for public transport or fuel and parking five days per week is $50.[6] Another $5 each day because the average Australian likes to arrive at work with a coffee to start the morning – that's $25 each week. Add another $30 for buying lunch two or three times a week. That's about $21 a day an employee can save by being able to work from home. Over the course of a year, if an

---

6   Yes, I know . . . there aren't many places where you can park this cheaply for a day, but I want to keep it low.

employee starts working from home full time, that could add up to $5,000. Fancy saving for a holiday?

Overall, working from home means happier employees, producing better work outcomes and who are financially better off. But don't take my word for it. It's all been reported. Research conducted for a report to the Fair Work Commission in late 2020 found that people reported the following benefits:

- no commute (89%)
- greater flexibility (68%)
- financial savings (65%)
- more time with family and friends (48%)
- increased productivity (42%).[7]

So, now we know working from home works for employees – what about businesses?

## ADVANTAGES FOR BUSINESSES

People start businesses for a whole range of reasons, but fundamentally it comes down to three things: purpose, time and money. Perhaps you started a business because you believed that as a business owner you could make a real difference to the world and the people you serve. Perhaps you believed that you would have more flexibility over your time to be able to spend more of it with your family or doing the things you love and less time stuck in the office from nine to five. Or perhaps you believed that being the business owner would mean a greater chance for financial gain as opposed to the limitations brought about by being hostage to a salary.

---

7 'Key Working from Home Trends Emerging from COVID-19 – A Report to the Fair Work Commission', Dr John Hopkins and Professor Anne Bardoel, Swinburne University of Technology, November 2020. © Commonwealth of Australia (Fair Work Commission) 2020. (www.fwc.gov.au/documents/sites/clerks-work-from-home/research/am202098-research-reference-list-su-241120.pdf).

Whatever your reason, having a Homeforce can help you reach your goal.

For me, it was all of these things, but the biggest goal was time. When I started my business five years ago I had three children aged six, three and one. Up until that point, in between maternity leave periods, I'd been working three days a week for a large law firm in Perth – plus whatever extra time I needed to work on the 'non-work' days to ensure the work was done and the clients and boss were happy.

Although I enjoyed quite a lot of flexibility given my long years of service with this firm, I was tired of needing to ask to come in late to attend an assembly at my daughter's school, or managing the difficulty of always making sure that daytime or after-school activities were always on my non-workday. I also wanted to move to the regions. I wanted the ability to plan my work around my life.

It doesn't always work out, but I definitely feel that I have managed to acquire the flexibility for family time that I was looking for when I started my business.

I've found that having a distributed team with the same goal of flexibility and freedom of time has created a close-knit team. We are all conscious of getting the work done in a way that enables us to have the lives we want.

## More money in your pocket

Whatever your reason for starting a business, unless you are making a profit you don't have a business. You might have just made yourself a job with a salary. And possibly a salary that is less than you could earn elsewhere. Also – making money means you are serving lots of clients and achieving your business purpose, and you can use that money to buy back your time by hiring staff and otherwise improving business operations. So money is often at the root of providing you those other benefits of business as well.

So how does a distributed team help you make money?

## Productivity increases

A range of research shows that employees who are happy at work, paid well and getting the required mix of autonomy, mastery and purpose, and are not distracted by their peers and office politics, are more likely to report themselves as more (or at least equally) productive when working remotely.[8] In research conducted in Australia in 2020, 77% of respondents found that working from home improved productivity, and in another research project over 90% of managers in the Australian public service believed their teams' productivity was the same or even higher when working from home.[9]

In the case of Lazer Safe, a manufacturing company based in Western Australia, remote work options have provided an extremely important degree of flexibility. With all of the business's customers based outside of Australia (mostly in Western Europe), working from home functionality has allowed employees to better manage critical issues/assignments.

Being able to work from anywhere in the world has also been extremely important for engineering staff and customer management staff who are required to travel, as it has allowed them to keep assignments progressing even when they weren't in the office.

This is all a big plus for productivity and customer satisfaction.

---

8   NSW Innovation and Productivity Council 2020, NSW Remote Working Insights: Our experience during COVID-19 and what it means for the future of work, Council Research Paper, Sydney, 2020.

9   'Preferences for flexible working arrangements: before, during and after COVID-19 – A Report to the Fair Work Commission', Professor Marian Baird AO and Daniel Dinale, University of Sydney, November 2020 (www.fwc.gov.au/documents/documents/awardmod/variations/2020/am202098-research-report-bd-301120.pdf).

More productive team members mean better work, and/or more work in less time. Each of these means more money in the door as the business is able to serve more clients, and those clients are more likely to return due to higher levels of service satisfaction.

Some of you might not believe this. You may have personally experienced remote teams working at lower levels of productivity. If that's the case, are you basing this on the experience of a random one-off day of remote work? Or based on the forced experience of working from home during the pandemic?

To be blunt – neither of those are good examples of what it is truly like to have a distributed team. In the first case, it may have been an employee wanting a day off for a personal reason so they had a 'working from home' day. Or perhaps they were an already disengaged team member.

In the second case – I think it is unfair to judge the productivity of all distributed teams based on the results achieved during the pandemic. Surveyed workers working remotely during the pandemic mostly judged themselves as being more productive, although many said their productivity didn't change and others said they were less productive. But it makes sense that some were less productive, doesn't it? Many of us were simultaneously dealing with closed schools and the need to suddenly become teachers. Or barking pets. Or sharing a home office with our partners. We hadn't had the time to set up our ideal home office with all of the tools we would usually have access to. Our systems weren't designed to function with a distributed team. We were changing the rules as we went along.

At the College of Law, productivity increases came from perhaps unexpected sources.

Having always been a distributed team with multiple offices across Australia, the move to a complete work from home arrangement during the majority of 2020 meant that all employees across Australia and New Zealand were now on an equal playing field. They were all at home and communicating online. There was no barrier due to being part of the Sydney office, or the Perth office, or another office.

As Ann-Maree David, Executive Director, described, online video calls led to team members having a 'bird's eye view' into each others' lives. Seeing dogs, children and what home environments looked like created a more intimate connection between employees which helped improve communication.

The sense of 'we're all in this together' also led to increased collegiality. People were keen to share solutions they had uncovered with their colleagues across the country, opening the door on a greater sharing of information between the different 'offices' than had existed before.

Another factor that improves productivity is a reduction in presenteeism, which leads to an overall reduction in absenteeism. We've all fallen victim to the office cold which has spread like wildfire, taking down one worker at a time because some person decided to come to work when they should've stayed home. Without the need to be at the office – whether because there is work that just has to be done, or because to not be in the office is career suicide – we see an awful lot less absence due to illness.

Giving people more flexibility as to where they work allows them to avoid the need to attend the office when it would be better for everyone if they didn't.

## Improved bottom line

Financial gain is not always about increasing revenue. Talk to any accountant and one of the first things they will ask you to do is review your expenses to see where you can make changes. Creating a Homeforce is a great way to do this.

First there is the obvious – less staff in the office means you need less space. By having 50% of your staff working from home at any one time, you can probably shave off at least 30% to 50% of your office rental requirements. That's a huge saving right there. It also gives you the opportunity to consider how you are using your space and to redesign it to better suit the purpose of collaboration rather than focused work. Maybe you can save even more by moving your whole business to a co-working space. The opportunities are endless.

A few years ago, well before the pandemic, Professor Nicholas Bloom from Stanford completed a two-year study which proved the incredible productivity boost that can come from work from home arrangements. Bloom studied Chinese company Ctrip – the largest travel agency in China – while it conducted a work from home trial with a view to making long-term savings on rental costs. Bloom helped Ctrip create a hybrid workforce with a group of volunteers working from home. The expectation of the study was that the company would save a lot of money on rental space, but would take a hit on productivity.

That's not what happened. They did save a heap of money on rent – the equivalent of about $2000 per employee – but the real financial benefits came in less obvious results. Those working at home initially increased their productivity by 13%. By the end of the study there was an overall 24% increase in productivity because some volunteers decided to go back to working in the office, and only those who truly wanted to work remotely were still doing it.

This equated to about an additional day of productivity per week. Much of this was attributed to the fact that they were working a full shift – with their arrival at work not being dependent on public transport, there was no leaving early, and they were better able to concentrate at home. Also – sick days decreased and quit rates dropped by 50%. This meant a huge saving on recruitment and training costs.[10]

These kinds of savings are significant and shouldn't be easily dismissed.

In Australia, a report done in late 2020 by Boston Consulting Group found that nearly half of the 120 Australian businesses surveyed were expecting to reduce their office space by mid 2022.[11] Will you be one of them?

### Decreased staff turnover

Another less obvious cost saving is that brought on by employee loyalty. Employees who want flexibility and aren't getting it with you will likely leave if their expectations aren't being met. Distributed and hybrid teams are the way of the future. You will start to lose staff and find it difficult to attract quality staff if you aren't offering what people are looking for and have come to expect. You will need to mind the expectation gap before it leads to relationship issues.

Workers who choose to work remotely are motivated by that choice and are more likely to be loyal to an employer that provides it. Loyal team members are less likely to go out looking for another job, just like with Ctrip in the story above. Who needs an extra $5k a year if it means having to commute to an office and being bound to nine to five again?

---

10 Nicholas Bloom, 'Go ahead, tell your boss you are working from home', TED Talk.
11 'The Expectation Gap in the Future of Work', Boston Consulting Group, 14 December 2020 (www.bcg.com/en-au/publications/2020/understanding-the-expectation-gap-in-the-future-of-work-australia).

Reducing the numbers of staff leaving brings your turnover costs down – costs that are often not properly accounted for on a profit and loss statement. It's one thing to record the cost of a recruitment service or placement fee, but what about your time participating in that recruitment process, or training people in their new role, or helping them integrate with the rest of the team? It is very hard to put a figure on those costs. Some research suggests that the cost to the bottom line each time you need to replace a staff member is as much as 33% of the employee's base salary.[12]

Loyal employees are also more likely to speak positively about the business – and we all know that word of mouth and reputation can mean everything in business. Not only can it help bring in more business, it can also help you find your next team member as the business grows.

This benefit worked against me recently. We were recruiting for another lawyer to join our team and found a great candidate living in another capital city but who was planning to move to Perth. Just as we were getting to the end of the recruitment process she withdrew. Why? Because when her current employer found out she was looking to resign they offered her the ability to work completely remotely and didn't even mind if she moved States in order to keep her employed. This kind of action by employers always impresses me. They saw a star performer they wanted to keep, and they allowed themselves to think outside the box to do it.

---

12  Work Institute, USA.

## Winning the war on talent

That brings me to the next benefit for businesses – quality staff. If your current team members are out there spreading the word about how wonderful a place to work your business is, you are more likely to attract a higher number of applicants for any available positions. Often the next staff member can be sourced from within the contacts of your existing staff – meaning they are already pre-vetted. A lot of firms use referral schemes – but loyal, happy employees won't need cash to motivate them to recommend a person join your business if they truly believe it is a great place to work. Also – no staff member will want to introduce someone into the team who doesn't fit your team culture. Why would they take the risk of ruining a good thing?

Another benefit of a Homeforce is that you aren't limited to the people who live within a two-hour radius of your office. This increases your pool of applicants exponentially and means you truly can get the best person for the job – no matter where they live. When advertising our open positions, we've had applications from across Australia and from as far away as Norway.

You might even purposefully choose to hire someone who lives on the other side of the country (or world) in order to increase the working hours available in your business. How wonderful would it be to finish your working day by sending a job to a team member around the world, and find that when you return the next day that job is already completed and waiting for you?[13]

---

13  A word of caution here. Employing someone who lives in another country is not as simple as just finding them and having them agree. You will need to ensure you comply with any local employment laws and tax laws as well as meet Australian requirements. If you are looking to go 'global' with your workforce, take some time to get some advice how to do it lawfully.

## Improved diversity

Diversity has gained increased recognition for being a key component to continued business success. McKinsey & Company found that gender diverse companies are 15% more likely to outperform non-gender diverse companies, and ethnically diverse companies are 35% more likely to outperform non-ethnically diverse companies.[14]

We now have five different generations at work. From the Traditionalists, to the Baby Boomers, Gen X, Millennials (Gen Y) and the youngest, Gen Z. We also have more women working than ever before, dual income families, and more people balancing caring and working responsibilities. It's been commonly known that mothers have been keen for remote work opportunities, but many women have been reluctant to take them due to the understanding that 'face time' was necessary in order to have a real place in a team and for career advancement.

Creating a Homeforce is a way to better service these changing labour pool patterns. Whether it is the stereotypical introverted Gen Z, a working parent, or an older person transitioning to retirement, each have different reasons for wanting to work from home. Adding this to the ability to hire ethnically diverse people living around the globe, a Homeforce allows the creation of a diverse team in a truly global way.

## Future proofing the business

The world of work has changed at lightning speed over the last 100 years, and there doesn't seem to be any signs of it slowing down. Whether you look at the increase in use of technology, the increase in numbers of people in the workforce − particularly women − or the types of work that we perform, the changes have been intense.

---

14 McKinsey & Company, 2015, 'Why Diversity Matters', viewed 10 August 2016, www.mckinsey.com/business-functions/organization/our-insights/whydiversity-matters.

Businesses need to be alert to changes and ready to innovate to meet new trends or be left behind.

One benefit I have heard over and over again from business owners is that the coronavirus pandemic forced them to move fast on technological innovation that they had been stalling on implementing. Teams that had been talking about trying out Zoom, Teams or other video-conferencing software were forced to implement it overnight as they moved to work from home.

Creating a Homeforce requires business owners and their team members to continue to innovate using technology. By being placed in an environment where use of tech is the norm, there is less fear and avoidance and more willingness to try something new, which will help productivity and build resilience to aid business continuity.

## UNEXPECTED BENEFITS

### Introverts become more comfortable

I recently spoke with Ann-Maree David, Executive Director of the College of Law, about the benefits she has seen from implementing working from home arrangements with her team. We discussed all the usual ones, and then she said something that really grabbed my attention: 'The more introverted people who usually sit back during a meeting are more willing to speak up.' In a formal interview with her recently, Ann-Maree addressed this further and suggested that it may be due to the lack of ease in a distributed team to call a spur-of-the-moment meeting. There is no more just grabbing people as you poke your head into their office. Instead, meetings are generally planned more in advance and agendas prepared and circulated, giving all people time to think and be ready to participate.

Also, perhaps being on the other end of a camera has allowed a greater number of people to contribute their thoughts and ideas during meetings, as opposed to them being dominated by the usual extroverts who are happy to jump in. Although there is no research on this yet, I'd hazard a guess that it has something to do with the fact these people are all safe in their own home working environment. Introverts are happiest when in their own space with time to think, so being in a shared meeting room physically surrounded by people is physically draining and less likely to promote participation.

### It's good for the environment

Let's not forget the environment. The reduction in commuting doesn't just mean more time for those people to do other things, it means lower emissions. The individual who doesn't need to drive to work reduces their emissions, and the people who do have to drive to work can get there quicker with reduced road congestion, which also reduces emissions.

One of the amazing positive stories I heard about during a coronavirus lockdown period in Perth, Western Australia, was a life that was saved because an ambulance wasn't stuck in freeway congestion.

Let's also not forget how remote working helps encourage the paperless office. Without easy access to a big photocopier, and with a reduced need to drop printed copies of documents on other people's desks, it becomes a lot easier to teach people how to manage without doing a lot of printing.

\* \* \*

Creating a distributed team isn't just good for our businesses and our employees, it also has the potential to have a very real positive impact on our environment and community.

All of these benefits combined have the impact of improving your reputation – not only in the eyes of your current workforce, but in the eyes of potential talent and your clients.

What's most exciting to you? Are you ready to jump in and take advantage?

We are all different, so each of us will respond more or less to each of these benefits.

Here's a handy summary to keep in mind.

**Benefits of remote work**

| Individuals | Companies |
|---|---|
| Save time - no more commute, so more personal time | Save money |
| Location independent - have your own 'corner office' | More productive employees = more profit |
| More choice of employer | Turnover and absenteeism down |
| Save money | Improved reputation |
| Can be more engaged and productive | Wider talent pool |
| | Greater diversity in employees |
| | Future-proofed business |
| | More input from introverts |

## A REALITY CHECK

Of course it's not all roses. There are obviously some challenges, or everybody would be doing it and I wouldn't be writing this book. The first one of course is to answer the question – is remote work even possible?

## CHAPTER 2

# Not all jobs, or people, can function from home

'What people have the capacity to choose, they have the ability
to change.'
Madeleine Albright

Let's not be ridiculous here. I'm not trying to argue that *all* jobs can be done by someone working from home. Not at the moment, anyway! We still need people to drive the garbage trucks that collect our household rubbish, people on production lines packing food or overseeing machines in case of breakdowns, and people in the pool with our children while they are learning to swim.

However, there are a great many jobs that can be worked from home. Some are obvious – like all the knowledge worker jobs such as lawyers and accountants – and some may need a little out-of-the-box thinking. As I've mentioned earlier – remote working doesn't require every aspect of a job to be capable of being done remotely. The ultimate peak of the distributed Homeforce journey doesn't have to be your final goal. So long as some percentage can be worked remotely, the option is there to make it happen.

Once we've considered the jobs then we need to think about the people who are working them. There is no doubt that people will work better in an environment that is optimised for how they like to work. Some people like background music, some don't. Some like a clean desk, whereas others like to spread out. Some like the ability to frequently ask questions of their neighbours – while others are desperate for time on their own.

The trick here is that when creating a Homeforce you need to consider both the job to be performed, and also who is going to perform it. If a job can't be worked properly at home – any person you allow to do that is being set up to fail. On the other hand, the job might be fine to be worked from home, but the person chosen may not be suitable. Either way – the outcome won't be good for your business.

So, how do we make sure we are set up for success?

## IT'S NOT FOR ALL JOBS

It is clear that some jobs definitely can't be worked from home, some can, and others fall somewhere in between. In order to work out where on the spectrum a particular job falls you need to analyse exactly what it is that is required of a person performing that role. You need to do a job analysis looking at the tasks of the role, the responsibilities, how it relates to other jobs and the conditions required to optimally perform the role.

**Remote-work-ready continuum**

←--------------------------------------------------------------→

**Fully remote**                                                     **On site**

A good starting point is a job description. A job description lists all the essential and desirable skills of the person in the role, reporting and management responsibilities and the tasks to be undertaken by the employee. If you have job descriptions for the positions in your business, take the time now to pull them out and read them.

But don't stop there.

To truly analyse the fit for work from home, you need to go beyond a job description (when was the last time you reviewed that anyway?) and look at the reality. Does the current person in the role actually do all of the tasks on the list? Has the role evolved to a higher level since the job description was created or last updated? Have some tasks been delegated to another person or become redundant? Can they be automated? What conditions are needed to complete the tasks? What tools are required? Are they available outside an office environment? How do the individual tasks of the job holder interact with other employees and their tasks? Can all of the tasks be done at any time of the day? Or is it important that they are done at specific times – perhaps because of other tasks, or perhaps because they require input from other employees?

Also consider the amount of time spent on each activity. A job description can list a wide range of tasks, but some might be daily, or once a week, and others once a year. It is the regular tasks that are particularly relevant in deciding whether a job is suitable to be worked from home.

Gallup research[15] indicates that there are three criteria to call a role optimal for remote work:

1.  Employees can perform their duties away from the site.

2.  Most of the tasks or processes are clearly defined.

3.  The role doesn't require highly interdependent work for success.

Consider each of your roles against these criteria. But remember, just because a role doesn't meet all of these criteria, or it doesn't score 100% on a particular factor, doesn't mean the role can't be worked remotely. It may just need a little more planning and perhaps some additional support from the business and the individual's team.

---

15 'Working remotely: Careers, Management and Strategy'.

And watch out for any unconscious bias getting in the way. For example, doctors. Most of us assume doctors need to see us in person, touch us and look closely at us to do their job well. But look how far telehealth has come. Okay, you may not be able to have your broken arm mended over the internet, but most people have home thermometers and can answer a bunch of questions about their health over a phone or video call. So, doctors definitely fall in a range of places on the remote-work-ready continuum.

What about the role of receptionist? Surely that must be in-person only? Well – not necessarily.

A standard receptionist position description may state that the receptionist needs to answer the phone and greet visitors. However, the question has to be asked, how often are they greeting visitors? Is it always the receptionist greeting them – or do they have other responsibilities that often mean the person who is meeting with the visitor will greet them?

What about the phones? Phone systems have changed in amazing ways in the last 20 years, and it is now super easy to transfer telephone numbers to other phones, have a phone system purely run through the internet, and have fabulous automated messaging that doesn't require a receptionist full time. Can a receptionist be at home managing the phone service?

As you can see, what would typically be thought of as a position that must absolutely be done in the office often actually falls somewhere in between on the spectrum.

**Remote-work-ready continuum**

$\longleftarrow$-------------------------------------------------------$\longrightarrow$

| **Fully remote** | | **On site** |
|---|---|---|
| e.g. Lawyer, | Receptionist | Pilot |
| Admin assistant, | Doctor | Manufacturing |
| Psychologist | | Bricklayer |

As you can see, you need to have a thorough understanding of the role before you can even begin to think about how it will translate to a distributed arrangement, taking into account the three Gallup criteria listed above. It's also important to ensure that any assessment considers the team as a whole and the impact of moving one or more roles to a distributed work model. In part II we will look at doing a job analysis in detail as we move through the framework.

Remember it doesn't need to be an all-or-nothing decision. A position doesn't have to be either work from home on a full-time basis, or not. In many cases your staff may just be wanting to work from home some of the time. Hybrid is definitely the way of the future. Perhaps you just want to work out how positions can be modified to be worked from home for certain periods of time, or for emergency situations like another pandemic (please no!).

Don't limit your thinking with outmoded ideas. Challenge stereotypes to truly see how you can create a Homeforce that's right for you.

## IT'S NOT FOR EVERYONE

The speed at which the coronavirus pandemic unfolded didn't really allow us time to consider whether or not a particular person was suited to work from home. For most businesses, it was simply a case of, 'Quick – everyone grab a laptop and start working at home!' We were in the office one day and at home the next. We didn't have the luxury of considering individual suitability.

If we did consider suitability, it was more in the context of wondering about the person's family life and home capacity. Were there young children in the house who were going to be distracting?

I think the whole world remembers the man who was giving an interview on BBC television when his young daughter opened the home office door and casually strolled in. She was closely followed by his other child wheeling through in a walker. Seconds later his wife came running in. Her desperation to capture the children and escape without being seen was palpable. Of course, all this was captured on BBC television and quickly went viral.[16]

In pre-pandemic times this was a notable event. Now, kids and animals crashing zoom meetings is an everyday occurrence, and only the most exceptional will rate sharing on social media.

Or maybe your suitability thoughts went to questions like: Was there a partner/housemate who was also going to be working from home and needing to share the office space? Was there sufficient internet capacity?

Little thought was able to be given to the individual nature of the person themselves.

Unfortunately, this is where many work from home arrangements can fall down. It is usually easy enough to source a desk, computer and internet connection, but it is much harder to change someone's personal characteristics.

### The personality traits of a good remote worker

If you do a Google search for personality traits of a good remote worker you'll see words like:

---

16  If you fancy a laugh, check out the video here: https://www.youtube.com/watch?v=Mh4f9AYRCZY.

According to some research conducted by Work/Life Strategist Dr Bailey Bosch in about 2019,[17] to be a good remote worker requires three characteristics – conscientiousness, emotional regulation and influence:

- **Conscientiousness** is the ability to be positive, keen and self-motivated. If an employee is going to be working from home they need to be able to GSD (get stuff done) without having their peers physically present or a manager standing over them as an accountability tool. They need to be able to create their own positive energy instead of relying on the energy that is created when a group of people are brought together for a common purpose, like in an office space. Without this an employee may struggle to get themselves to turn their computer on in the morning, may be easily distracted by the latest Netflix series or spend way too long making and enjoying lunch in their home kitchen.

- **Emotional regulation** is the ability to have a proactive approach to your own personal wellbeing. Almost the opposite problem to not having enough conscientiousness, if an employee can't emotionally regulate, they may forget to care for themselves adequately. For example, they may forget to take breaks as they aren't subtly inspired by other staff around them getting up to make cups of tea or taking a lunch break. In the legal industry we have a long-established practice of taking a lunch break from 1 p.m. till 2 p.m. to match with the Court closure. There will always be people working through or eating lunch at their desk, but it gets super quiet and everyone knows it is time for a break. Forgetting to take a break can lead to a heightened sense of stress and ultimately health problems. Also, without the day-to-day office interactions it can be easy to start to feel lonely and isolated.

---

17  www.abc.net.au/news/2019-09-23/three-traits-that-tell-if-you-are-suited-to-working-from-home/11531924.

Loneliness is a real issue. Research undertaken at Swinburne University in 2020, found that 29% of people surveyed noted loneliness as one of their big challenges with remote work. Feeling lonely and left out can reduce our happiness and productivity and lead to long-term health concerns. It is therefore super important that an employee is conscious of their own health and able to manage their mental and physical fitness to ensure wellbeing.

- **Influence** is the ability to be able to quickly connect with others and make effective relationships. It is an obvious outcome of increased working from home arrangements that employees have less physical contact with others, and fewer ad hoc connections. For example, you can't just turn to the person next to you and ask them a question about what's on your screen. You won't accidentally bump into someone in the bathroom, kitchen or stairwell and strike up a random conversation about the weather or latest office gossip.

  All of these small interactions build over time to create relationships between the people around the office. When a person is working from home they need to be able to rely on other strategies to connect and build the relationships that are necessary for effective working dynamics. All too often it is easy for people working from home to not have any interactions with their team as they just put their head down and GSD. However, in many cases, team interaction is necessary for optimal business performance, and is also important to help the employee with their emotional regulation.

If you look back at that word cloud earlier, many of the words – like self-motivated, driven, disciplined and independent – are related to the need for conscientiousness. That's why I addressed it first above. However, there's a risk that someone who is high on conscientiousness may also, when under stress, have higher levels of anxiety. (Sounds like way too many lawyers I know.)

Since the pandemic Dr Bosch has had a chance to reconsider the research and apply the learnings she has as a result of working with many more people taking up remote work. In an interview I conducted with her in 2021, she explained that she now describes the ideal person suited to a distributed work arrangement as someone who fits the definition of a 'self-manager'. Interestingly she sees a lower level of need for 'influence' as more businesses are mindfully creating and implementing policies and procedures to ensure appropriate levels of communication between individuals and teams and to maintain culture. It's not just being left for the few random employees working remotely to make or break.

It's also been thought that introverts would be best at remote working as it is commonly believed they don't have the same level of need for human interaction as extroverts. However, it's not that simple. Even the greatest extrovert may find too many Zoom meetings overwhelming. As Dr Bosch said in our interview, the key is ensuring people have a bit of self-awareness so that they can take personal responsibility. For example, if an extrovert isn't getting enough interaction during their work life, perhaps they can look at how they may get that interaction in other ways in their personal life.

Other research has found that the most meaningful trait to predict whether someone will adapt to remote work is agreeableness.[18] The more they have of this, the better they will be as a collaborator and colleague in a remote environment as they are better able to maintain positive relationships due to their friendly and optimistic nature.

---

18 'The Implications of Working Without an Office', Ethan Bernstein, Hayley Blunden, Andrew Brodsky, Wonbin Sohn, and Ben Waber, *Harvard Business Review*, 15 July 2020 (hbr.org/2020/07/the-implications-of-working-without-an-office).

In short, there is no one trait that is going to mean a person will be good at remote work. However, there are clearly things we can look for when assessing whether a person is suited to working remotely.

## USING PERSONALITY TESTING

So how do we work out whether a person has the traits necessary to be successful in a remote work arrangement? One option is a personality test. There are a range of psychometric tests that have been developed over time – often referred to as 'personality tests'. Some of the most famous include the Myers–Briggs test and the DiSC Profile. One of my personal favourites is the Clifton Strengths Test developed by the Gallup Institute.

There are many others, all with widely varying degrees of academic research support, constantly popping up on the internet. Personality quizzes are often shared on social media as everyone seems to want to learn about themselves, or prove to themselves that they are the kind of person they think they are. The more creative the more shareable they are. Things like 'Which character are you?' or 'What's your spirit animal?'

One of my personal favourites of these creative tests is the 'My Creative Type' test created by Adobe. The names are cute, but even better – the graphics and animation are amazing. If you're curious I've done the Adobe test multiple times and I tend to show up as Visionary or Innovator. The common theme – I love creating ideas.

Tests are definitely a useful starting point, however I've never been 100% certain about them. Whenever I do one of these kinds of tests, I always feel like some things are right, but others not so much. I end up taking the test two or three times trying to see if I get a different result that feels a bit more 'me'. Anyone else want to admit to this?

The fact is that personality isn't permanent. There's a great book with exactly this title by Benjamin Hardy PhD. In that book Benjamin debunks the idea that we are stuck with our personality and shares his research about the fact that personality changes over time. He shares how we can intentionally choose to change through learning, changing our environment, goal setting and other personal transformation strategies.

So just because you struggled to work from home at one point in your life doesn't mean that you won't be fabulous at it later. For example, before kids I think I would really have struggled to work from home. I enjoyed being part of a big workforce, sitting in an area with my team and being able to have ad hoc face-to-face conversations. I loved all of that human interaction and the energy that came to me by being surrounded by loads of people all the time. Yet now, in my forties, my time is much more precious to me. I don't want to waste time sitting on public transport or in my car, and I don't have time for as much chat during office hours because I need to get my work done and get back to my family.

The lesson in this is choose a test that you consider is best suited to determining suitability of a candidate for a working from home role. However, don't let it be your only consideration. These tests aren't failproof. That's why there are so many of them. Use it as a guide only. You need to speak with the individual and get their feelings about the test results, where they think the test might be wrong or not taking into account relevant information. Speak to them about the role, their home life and their personality and do your best to match up all three. A test can help kick start these conversations so that you can identify specific individual challenges and what support may be required to set them up for success. As my friend Chris says, 'We all deserve the opportunity to learn new ways.' Unfortunately, there is no simple answer, and trying to find one is just setting yourself up to fail. So don't try.

It's also very important to consider individual preferences. Some people might be a great fit for your company, but don't want to be part of your Homeforce. They want to work in an office – at least some of the time.

Preferences may differ based on family life, home location compared to the office, where they feel most productive, length of employment with your company, how much enjoyment and beneficial experience they get from interacting with team members in the office and other personal factors.

## RESPONDING 'NO' TO A REQUEST – LEGALLY

Sometimes it is not the employer who starts the movement towards a remote arrangement. In fact, in Australia, up to now (aside from the avalanche of requests – or orders! – to work from home during the pandemic) the majority of work from home requests have been from women with caring responsibilities.

A request for a working from home arrangement will usually arise from one of two scenarios. First will be an employee who has been with you in the office for a while, and you are familiar with their work and personality. The other will be the situation where you are recruiting for a new staff member and the person you want to hire is keen to work from home.

Arguably the first situation is the easier one to deal with as there are fewer unknown quantities. You know the person, how they work, and they already have relationships with other team members and clients. However, you still don't know for sure how they will work from home.

If you get a request in either of these scenarios, and you hadn't previously made a decision that a job was suitable to be worked remotely, then it's important to know your underlying legal obligations before you start to consider whether or not a job or person is suitable for a remote work arrangement. Any decision, and how you communicate that decision, needs to comply with legal requirements.

## Don't discriminate

In Australia people (employees and potential employees) are protected from discrimination on the grounds of race, colour, sex, sexual orientation, age, physical or mental disability, marital status, pregnancy, religion, political opinion, family or carer's responsibilities and national extraction or social origin.

This means, for example, that you can't refuse a person's request to work from home because they are of a certain political persuasion, or because they have a young family.

## Be aware of your potential bias

For many people there is a natural instinct to say 'no' to a remote work request. Often this comes from some of the perceived challenges of remote work – like lack of collaboration and visibility over work performance.

However, I challenge you when you receive a request to imagine that the person asking is your star performer. If they are a great employee and super productive, what would you say to them? How far would you go to keep them happy and engaged?

If you would say 'yes' to the request, the challenge for you is to ask yourself why you are saying no to the individual in front of you. Is it because you don't like them? You don't think they are a good performer, or you don't trust them to work out of your sight?

If it's performance concerns, then that requires a specific conversation with the individual. If it's not, then what do you need to do or change to be able to grant that request?

It's also a good idea to involve other people in the decision making. A cross section of people who are affected (or even a complete outsider) will provide a greater perspective and limit any potential for bias.

## Flexible working arrangements – existing employees

In Australia, there are also special entitlements for employees who have been employed for at least 12 months and are covered by the National Employment Standards (NES). Those employees are legally entitled to request a flexible working arrangement from their employer if they fit into one of the following categories:

- are age 55 or older
- are a parent/carer of children school aged or younger
- are a carer
- have a disability
- are experiencing violence from a member of their family, or are caring or supporting a member of their immediate family or household who requires care or support because they are experiencing violence from their family.[19]

If you have an employee who fits into one of these categories and they have made a written request for a flexible arrangement, you need to make sure that you provide a written response within 21 days. You are only entitled to refuse the request on reasonable business grounds, and you must inform the employee of the reasons. Reasonable business grounds can include, among other things:

- cost of implementing the arrangement
- interruption to business services
- affect on other team members.

---

19 Please note, these flexible work provisions only apply to employers covered by the *Fair Work Act 2009* (Cth).

Therefore, all of the questions that we have looked at so far to help you determine if a job is suitable to be worked from home are important to consider when responding to a flexible work request.

The key with any request for flexible or remote working is to ensure that you remain open-minded. Take the example I shared earlier about our failed recruitment.

When our applicant for employment told her current employer that she was planning to move interstate and was looking at job opportunities, it would have been really easy for the employer to just give up on her and wait for her resignation. (Only five short years ago that is what happened to me, and I was only moving two hours away. But such was the lack of commitment to, and understanding of, remote working that nothing other than a resignation was going to work.)

Instead of giving up, the employer chose to do what is best for the business. It focused on the potential benefits. It considered alternatives, assessed the ramifications, and discussed those ideas and sought other options from the employee involved. Having open discussions about options and limitations is good for relationships and good for business.

## What if you say 'no' to an NES request?

There is no legal right in the *Fair Work Act 2009* (Cth) to appeal a refusal of an NES flexible working request to a statutory body such as the Fair Work Commission. However, an employee may have a right to appeal to someone else in your organisation if they've been given that right in a flexible work policy or a contract of employment. So be careful what rights you are establishing.

Also, depending on the reasons for saying no, an employee may have some other legal claims available. I've already mentioned discrimination, and there might also be general protections claims or unfair dismissal claims if a refusal leads to termination of employment.

One unfair dismissal claim arose when an employer refused to grant an employee's request to decrease working hours from 38 to 36 per week to care for his children. He wasn't happy and refused to comply with the direction to work his contracted 38 hours. His employer dismissed him for failure to comply with his contract and he brought an unfair dismissal claim. The Fair Work Commission agreed the refusal of the flexible work request led to the dismissal and therefore determined it was appropriate to review the decision. Ultimately, the FWC did find the employer had reasonable business grounds for the refusal, and so the unfair dismissal claim failed.[20]

### The lesson from the above case?

Just because you have these legal requirements doesn't mean you always have to say 'yes' when a request is made. Don't let fear of some kind of legal action stop you from making the right decision for your business. Fundamentally, if you have made your decision to refuse a working from home request on reasonable business grounds (and met other legal obligations), don't fear. It all comes down to what is suitable and practical in the circumstances.

---

20   *Tawasoly v Alpha Flight Services Pty Ltd* [2017] FWC 813.

CHAPTER 3

# Common challenges

'Nothing is impossible, the word itself says "I'm possible"!'
Audrey Hepburn

So far we've learned about the benefits of creating a Homeforce, and the importance of applying some rational thinking to whether or not particular jobs — and people — are suited to working from home. If you've come this far and building a Homeforce is definitely for you, it's important to have a good hard look at the challenges you will face while changing the way you operate your business.

Because there will be challenges.

Generally speaking, people are resistant to change. We all love being in our comfort zone. The place where we know ourself, the people around us, and there is no fear of being challenged. In building a Homeforce you will be stepping outside your comfort zone, and likely pushing your team out of their comfort zones — ready or not.

The key to overcoming any challenge is understanding as much about it as possible. Learn about the challenges, prepare for all known eventualities and maintain awareness. Being prepared gives you time to become accustomed to what is expected during this change process and allows you to train your brain to focus on the positives not the negatives.

This chapter is going to take you through the seven key challenges that you will likely experience while creating a Homeforce, everything from the physical challenges of setting up home offices, to mental and physical safety considerations, to how you personally handle the change.

Before we get started – keep this in mind. Having you read these challenges is designed to have you acknowledge them and make you aware of them so you can prepare for them. But it is also possible that reading through them all now will leave you feeling like it is all just too hard. It's not. Creating a Homeforce is eminently doable, and I will walk you through how to overcome all of these challenges in part II of the book.

## CHALLENGE 1: ATTITUDE (YOUR MINDSET AND THE MINDSET OF YOUR TEAM AND CLIENTS)

### Your mindset

One of the biggest challenges in implementing any kind of change – especially one with such wide-reaching effects on many – is your own attitude towards it. Your mindset – one of the great buzzwords of the 2020s. But it's a buzzword for a good reason. It is fundamental to anything you want to accomplish. It's going to be a darn sight harder to leap over the hurdles if you don't believe you can do it.

It would be totally surprising if you haven't asked yourself one of these questions at least once:

- 'How will I know if my employees are really working?'

- 'How can I supervise their work?'

- 'How can I teach them properly how to do their jobs and follow the company systems and processes when they aren't there for me to show them?'

- 'What happens if something goes wrong in their home – am I legally responsible for it?'
- 'How are these team members going to integrate with each other when they don't get a chance to interact in person?'

And let's not forget about your possible worries about your clients:

- 'Will they like moving to video conferencing?'
- 'Will they miss visiting the office and start looking for another service provider?'

These sorts of questions lead to the wrong kind of thoughts. You might start hearing yourself saying, 'It's just too hard', or, 'There are too many things that can go wrong.' Negative thoughts like these are likely to lead you to a negative result – or no result at all. Your actions will be focused on confirming your beliefs – that a Homeforce is just too hard.

I sent out a survey in 2020 asking business owners about their experiences with working from home. One of my all-time favourite comments was a description of a negative experience being, *'Interruptions from less experienced staff as queries are either all written or via phone . . .which causes more interruptions compared to a five-second conversation.'*

I still haven't quite figured out why a phone call provides more interruption than what is expressed to be a five-second conversation in an office environment.

I saw this as a true example of a mindset that believed communicating over distance is hard, and it is always better face to face. With this mindset there was no way the business owner was going to think positively of using the telephone or video conferencing technology to complete the same task.

Building a Homeforce requires you to believe absolutely in the benefits that it can provide, and to be absolutely committed to working through the challenges. It is very tempting to fall back on old beliefs that team members need to be physically present to get maximum productivity out of them. This idea that people in the office are more productive than those outside it. However that kind of thinking won't give you the benefits we talked about at the beginning of this book: increased productivity, loyalty and financial gain to name a few.

As the champion of this business transformation, it's essential that you stay focused on the positives and ready to work through the challenges. You need to visualise the positive effects that can be generated from creating a Homeforce. Picture yourself and your team in this new way of operating and make it feel like a reality.

## Employee mindset

It's not just your own mindset that you need to influence and control. You also need to look at the other people involved in this transformation and how they are handling the change. The two greatest stakeholders will be your employees and your clients.

The biggest challenge you will likely confront from your employees is an extension of your own biggest fear: that all of your employees are just lazing around at home, watching Netflix and shopping online. When you translate this into a fear held by employees it becomes a concern that some of their team will be at home, watching Netflix and online shopping *and they will have to pick up the slack and do more work.*

No employee wants to think that their workload is increasing while their income remains the same and some other employee is getting a free ride. In fact – no Aussie would like that idea at all. It definitely doesn't match our strong belief in everyone getting a 'fair go'.

The obvious issue with these kinds of core beliefs is that the believers won't do anything to make the transition to a Homeforce easier. In fact, an even worse outcome will be those who are resistant to implementing the Homeforce transformation deliberately sabotaging it. Sabotage could take many forms – refusing to delegate work to remote workers or making it difficult for others to do so, telling clients the other team member is not available and taking over responsibility for the work, managers becoming micro-managers as they try to retain control, and so on. But the most common is likely to be gossiping with other team members about the supposed 'slackers'. This might start off with a few comments that appear harmless, but if left unchecked it can become a regular occurrence that leaves the employees on the receiving end feeling left out and bullied. All of this creates an 'us' and 'them' culture.

When you have a distributed team, maintaining a positive mindset among all team members is essential for building a strong morale and culture. As the champion of the Homeforce it will be up to you to help your team see, become a part of, and ultimately help build your vision.

## Client mindset

Let's not forget your clients. They are the other key stakeholder in your Homeforce transformation. Are the clients used to walking into your physical office premises to meet with your employees? Are they the type of people who are resistant to the use of technology such as video conferencing? Perhaps they like the ritual of walking in, being greeted and given coffee and biscuits, and shaking hands with a team member (if we ever get back to that post-pandemic). Will they be worried that staff working from home means a lower level of service?

If your clients have any of these concerns – how will you maintain adequate connection and communicate with them to prevent the fears leading them to find another provider? Or worse, having their fears of poor service become reality?

How will you sell the idea of a Homeforce to your clients? How do you make your clients a part of your new vision? And how do you stay mindful and positive in the wake of negativity from those around you – particularly those paying the bills?

There is a big difference between your own fears about what your clients want and expect, and the truth about what your clients want and expect.

It is very important to not get caught up in your own assumptions. The best thing to do? Talk to your clients. A novel idea for some. You could do an impersonal survey – and this might be best if you have a large volume of clients. But I recommend picking up the phone and getting some off-the-cuff comments too. It wouldn't be surprising if many are going through the same process and their personal experience can give you great insight.

## CHALLENGE 2: THE TOOLS

### Physical tools

During the coronavirus pandemic there was what you would call a 'rush' on home office supplies. Coincidentally, at the same time that many offices were starting to move their staff to working from home arrangements, I was trying to source a secondhand desk for my daughter's room. We had agreed to go secondhand to afford something bigger than we would be able to purchase brand new on our budget. It was impossible. Everything that was posted on Gumtree or Facebook marketplace was overpriced, and even still it sold rapidly.

My poor daughter had to wait until things started to return to normal in Western Australia; people returned to their usual offices and started selling off the desks they had purchased in a rush. Four months she waited! But it did mean that she ended up with a desk much newer than expected. You win some, you lose some.

Desks weren't the only supplies in hot demand. One person who completed my work from home survey commented that setting up a home office for her employees was one of her biggest business challenges in responding to the pandemic. She walked into Officeworks to purchase a keyboard to find only two left on the shelf – of any type of keyboard at all. Needless to say – she grabbed one and ran.

What else does an employee need? Assuming we are talking about a knowledge worker employee, then at the very least they will need a space to work in, a desk, comfortable chair, computer and an internet connection. Once we've listed the basics it's necessary to dig a little deeper about the quality of each of these things.

For example, is a one-metre-long desk sufficient? Do they like to work using a standing desk from time to time? What about the chair? Does the employee have a need for a specific kind of chair to support their back or some other physical condition? Can the employee work well with just a laptop – or do they need a big computer screen, or even two, to function efficiently?

Once you've considered all of these questions and worked out what your employees need – then we hit the million-dollar question. Who provides and who pays?

Setting up a home office can be an expensive business. Good desks and chairs aren't cheap, and we haven't even started to consider computers. So are you required to provide and pay for these tools? The answer to this is a typical lawyer answer – it depends. It depends on whether the person you are putting into your Homeforce is a current employee. It depends on whether the person has these items at home already and has room for any additional items. It depends on what you can negotiate.

During the coronavirus pandemic employers handled this concern in a variety of ways. Some had conversations with employees about what their home situation was and then determined what else the employee needed to function. For example, if they only had an iPad at home, they would send them home with their work desktop computer. For other employers, their concerns about security (we will get to that later) meant they required all staff to take their desktop computers home. The bigger companies even sent IT professionals to all employees' homes to ensure they were properly connected and operational.

If they didn't have a desk, and the kitchen table (or ironing board) wasn't a suitable option, they either delivered their work desk to their home or helped them purchase one. If the employee relied on their phone for internet data, the employer may have arranged and paid for home internet connection.

In the case of other businesses, the solution was offering a monthly allowance to an employee to compensate them for the costs of running a home office. I'm not just talking about the desk, chair and internet here. Obviously if you are using your home more there is more wear and tear on it, plus extra water usage, extra electricity, and so on. It can all add up. The pandemic was a special circumstance which led to some different results. Safety and public health orders pretty much required businesses to direct employees to work from home, which meant the question over the liability to provide and pay for home office equipment sometimes had a different answer.

Leaving the pandemic aside – if you are advertising a job as remote, or an employee approaches you wanting to go remote, there is no hard-and-fast rule saying you must pay and provide everything to make that happen. You've got much more capacity for a negotiated agreement. So, start with the physical things. List what is needed, decide who will provide them, and then decide whether any money will change hands. Like other aspects such as wages and holidays, this just becomes another part of the negotiation with the employee.

## Non-physical tools

Offices aren't just made up of physical things. Moving to a Homeforce means rethinking how some of your office processes work. For example, if you can't meet with your clients face to face, how do you conduct business? If you can't have weekly team meeting huddles in the office kitchen or meeting room, how do you communicate the weekly tasks and challenges?

If you can't sit in a room around a whiteboard, how do you collaborate? If you can't post a list of tasks on the wall, how do you communicate them?

One result of the pandemic was a lot more people using video conferencing. The shares for Zoom went through the roof. People started to learn what 'Teams' in their Office365 subscription was all about.

I've run a law firm with a distributed team since 2016. Launching the firm coincided with me moving to live two hours away from my capital city, so it wasn't as easy for me to visit clients at their premises or in cafés or co-working places when someone wanted to meet me physically.

I offered video conferencing or telephone consultations instead. The uptake on the video conferencing was pretty much zero. (I did a lot of driving in those early days. If you ever need a good podcast recommendation - let me know!)

Until the pandemic. All of a sudden everyone was forced to consider an alternative to the face-to-face meeting and I finally had a great uptake on my video conferencing option. In fact - even now when the Perth area is returning to normal (and I now live back in the city), many people are still selecting a video conference option. They've seen the light - I mean benefits. Video conferencing saves time, for them and for me.

This use of technology of course links back to the need for physical items. What do you do in the case of an employee whose computer doesn't have an inbuilt camera? (Webcams were another sold out item during the pandemic.) If you want your employees to participate via camera, are you responsible for sourcing one?

How about their internet connection? What kind of internet speed do they need to be able to connect to the company systems and operate effectively? There is nothing worse than a video connection that is constantly freezing. It may be that if your employee relies on their mobile phone to hotspot to their computer, a wired internet connection will need to be sourced to provide higher speed internet. Or perhaps it is the other way around and you will need a portable device to get high speed internet, and a higher data allowance.

Once you've considered the obvious changes, think a bit more widely. What about the office processes that you take for granted? Anyone still have a physical filing tray? If you run an office that still relies on a great deal of paper – you need another option. There may not be anyone in the office to file that paper. There also won't be any employees in the office generating that paper. But are they generating it at home? What are they doing with it there? Filing their own paper? Scanning and saving? Is that efficient – or necessary?

Maybe working from home will herald the use of new technology to remove paper from our lives. There are many businesses now that rely solely on tablets and stylus pens for creating handwritten notes that are automatically saved, and can be converted to Word for easy editing.

What software do you need? Are your usual programs cloud-based or able to be remote accessed in other ways? If not, what's the process and cost to establish that?

And how do you ensure your employees know how to use these new-fangled things? No one wants to become known as the business where the lawyer made the whole Courtroom listen to its hold music, or who had an employee who forgot to turn off their camera when they went to the toilet!

These issues get back to the question we asked earlier in the book – is this job a suitable one to be worked from home? You need to consider the entirety of a role, and how it fits in with the whole business, before you can make that decision with any degree of surety. All of the tools necessary to enable an employee to perform their job successfully must be considered: physical tools, technology tools and office systems and processes.

\* \* \*

The challenge for you is to consider all of these potential costs of running a Homeforce and make a decision about how you want to handle them. Do you provide everything? Do you provide some things and pay an allowance for others? Or perhaps you decide you want to pay nothing as the employee is making a gain from being able to be part of your Homeforce – they are already saving money (and time, which is more important to many) in not having to commute to the office.

Maybe you consider them paying the costs of a home set up is a fair exchange for the benefits they are receiving.

## CHALLENGE 3: PHYSICAL SAFETY

For many business owners, physical safety didn't even rate five minutes of their time while they were preparing their business to survive during the pandemic. Instead, they took a quick look around, identified those team members who sit at their computer all day, and sent them home with their laptop (if that). The thought was about business survival – how do we keep operational? – with little focus on the effect on individual employees.

For others, they may have considered safety briefly but taken the view that of course an employee is safe in their own home so there is nothing to consider further. Unfortunately, this is not always the case.

Once an employee is working from home, a portion of their home becomes a workplace. As an employer you are responsible for providing them with a safe place of work (as far as is reasonably practicable), and that now includes in their home.

Now for me, a safety hazard of working from home has been the easy access to the fridge, which I all too often stock full of chocolate. Did I mention that I can be a comfort eater when I'm feeling stressed? Obvious risks here – obesity and diabetes to name a couple. Perhaps somewhat outweighed by the benefit of getting up from my desk and walking to the fridge to get to that comfort food?

While I'm not totally joking about this being an issue for me (and others), there are much bigger issues to consider when thinking about safety in the home. We need to start by considering exactly what makes up the workplace.

For starters, it is not the whole home including all the rooms and yards. However, it's also not just the place where an employee's desk and computer are located.

It is any area that an employee needs to use and transverse in their ordinary working day – the office space where the desk is located (hopefully not the dining room table – not usually great from an ergonomic point of view), the kitchen area for lunch and drinks, and the bathroom area. All of these are essential. So is the pathway you need to travel to get between each of these rooms. The laundry, kids bedrooms and the like are not part of a normal working day and therefore don't make up the workplace.

Each of these spaces that makes up the workplace needs to be considered from a safety perspective. For example, those of us with young children know that kids seem to leave toys everywhere and it can definitely be a hazard worth watching out for. Ever walked on Lego blocks before? There's a reason why people make jokes about accidently stepping on Lego blocks being like walking on fire.

The most obvious hazard for knowledge workers – whether at home or in an office – is poor workspace set up. A 'desk' at the wrong height (such as the kitchen table), a chair that doesn't give good back support, lack of a footrest, keyboards and mouse that aren't suitable, height of computer screens – these are some of the factors that are looked at in an ergonomic assessment.

It's one thing to provide all of the right tools, but it is a totally separate matter to make sure that an employee is setting them up and using them correctly – especially when you don't have a visual overview of them each day.

Then there are less obvious hazards.

In 2016 a woman employed by the ABC in Canberra as a journalist was working from home. It was pretty common for her to work from home on occasion but there was no formal process for what days that might occur. On one particular day she decided to take a break from work around 9:30 a.m. and go for a run. Unfortunately for her, she had a case of bad luck and ended up falling and breaking her hip.

Unfortunately for her employer, as she was working from home on the day it occurred, she brought a workers compensation claim against her employer, arguing that the injury arose out of or in the course of her employment. So – the big question: was she successful? Well – no. But don't relax too quickly.

The Court said that if she had taken that run during her lunch break then the answer might have been different. Why? Because all she needed to prove was that on the day of the injury, her place of work was her home, and that the run occurred at a time that she was temporarily absent from her place of work during an ordinary recess in her employment – such as a morning tea or lunch break.

So, along with the main workstation set up, the walkways around the house, undertaking activity outside the house and the fridge (sort of joking) are all examples of potential safety hazards that an employee might experience while working from home. It is not enough to focus on the standard office hazards such as an ill-fitting chair, poor-quality computer screens or wrong desk height. As an employer, you need to give consideration to your employees' physical safety at home and make sure you have addressed any hazards. There needs to be a proper safety assessment that correctly identifies and manages risks.

**Other considerations**

Also – let's be real here. Some people working from home like to leave the home office environment and work at their local café. Or perhaps at a co-working space. Or even sitting at the local park. Maybe because their children have a pupil-free day at school and they need to go somewhere with fewer distractions. Sometimes going elsewhere, like a parent's house, is a necessity if internet or power goes out. Or maybe they just like getting out and about for a change of scenery and new inspiration. Are you going to ask your employee to disclose all of these possibilities before the remote work arrangement starts? How are you going to handle doing safety assessments on them all?

What about clients and other people? What if a client wants to meet with your employee and it's convenient for both to meet at the employee's home? Is that something you will allow? What if the client is injured tripping over something on the front driveway while walking to the front door? Who's responsible for that? What if your employee doesn't have home insurance? Or perhaps it wouldn't apply in any event. You don't want to be finding out when it's too late.

* * *

Dealing with the safety side of remote working from home requires a good deal of thought about the actual work environment, its hazards and how they can be mitigated. A remote work arrangement requires a balance between an employer's need to minimise risks and an employee's desire to live their life and work with as much flexibility and choice as possible.

## CHALLENGE 4: MENTAL SAFETY

There is no doubt that awareness of mental health issues in the workplace is at an all-time high. Research has shown beyond a doubt that there is a clear nexus between health and wellbeing and high-performance teams who are productive and effective.

In some recent research, one in five Australians (21%) had taken time off work in the past 12 months due to feeling mentally unwell. This statistic more than doubled (46%) where the person considered their workplace to be mentally unhealthy.[21] It is estimated that untreated mental health conditions will cost Australian workplaces approximately $10.9 billion per year. This is made up of about $4.6 billion in absenteeism, $6.1 billion in presenteeism, and $146 million in compensation claims.[22]

Research also shows that with leadership support, organisations implementing effective actions to create mentally healthy workplaces can expect a positive return on investment of 2.3. That is, for every dollar they spend on effective action, there is on average $2.30 in benefits gained. These benefits typically take the form of improved productivity by reducing absenteeism and presenteeism.[23]

Work can be challenging. Many of us already work in high-stress environments with the demands of clients and colleagues. Remote work doesn't remove the mental health risks that already exist in the workplace, like bullying. The question is, what about remote work provides any additional challenges?

A 2020 survey conducted by Swinburne University of Technology found that some of the most common challenges of remote work identified by participants were as shown in the graph opposite.

---

21 www.headsup.org.au/docs/default-source/resources/bl1270-report---tns-the-state-of-mental-health-in-australian-workplaces-hr.pdf?sfvrsn=8.

22 PwC. (2014) 'Creating a mentally healthy workplace: return on investment analysis'. Accessed online from www.headsup.org.au/docs/default-source/resources/beyondblue_workplaceroi_finalreport_ may-2014.pdf.

23 PwC. (2014) 'Creating a mentally healthy workplace: return on investment analysis'. Accessed online from www.headsup.org.au/docs/default-source/resources/beyondblue_workplaceroi_finalreport_ may-2014.pdf.

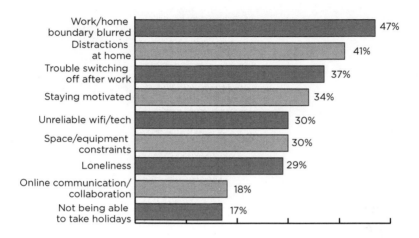

| | |
|---|---|
| Work/home boundary blurred | 47% |
| Distractions at home | 41% |
| Trouble switching off after work | 37% |
| Staying motivated | 34% |
| Unreliable wifi/tech | 30% |
| Space/equipment constraints | 30% |
| Loneliness | 29% |
| Online communication/collaboration | 18% |
| Not being able to take holidays | 17% |

As you can see, the vast majority of these focus on how the individual is feeling and thinking.

**Loneliness**

The 2020 'NSW Remote Working Insights' report listed the impact on opportunities to socialise and working relationships as the worst aspect of remote work for the 1500 people surveyed. This is not totally surprising given our innate need as humans for social connection. In fact, the world's longest study on adult development, conducted by Harvard, found that good relationships keep us happier and healthier, and living longer.[24] So watching out for loneliness and disengagement among your team is going to be a key challenge with a remote workforce.

---

24 'What Makes a Good Life? Lessons from the Longest Study on Happiness', by Robert Waldinger – TedX BeaconStreet. www.ted.com/talks/robert_waldinger_what_makes_a_good_life_lessons_from_the_longest_study_on_happiness?language=en.

Speaking from experience, working from home can feel lonely and isolating. For me, I would watch my husband leave for work, drop my children at school, and then sit down at the computer ready to work. In those first days of my business, it was just me. There were no employees or contractors to check in with. My only communications during the working day were with clients.

To start with I thought it was fine. I told myself that I had my conversations with clients as social connection, and that it would mean I was more productive at work without people to distract me.

Then I slowly started to realise that I was missing human interaction. I had gone from working in a business with over 200 staff to being a team of one. There was no one sitting at a desk next to me, no accidental meetings with colleagues (who had become friends) in the kitchen or bathroom or just traversing the halls. There were no group meetings to work on team projects, within or across practice areas. The only person I had to consult with was myself. I was lonely. And I started to get depressed. (Spoiler alert – it didn't stay that way.)

If feelings of isolation and disconnection are left undetected, the ultimate risk is that an employee will develop a mental health condition such as depression. In the shorter term it may lead to a decrease in productivity and lower quality work outcomes, resulting in poor service to clients and ultimately a decrease in business financial performance and possibly a workers compensation claim, and it can have a lasting effect on the individual employee.

No good business owner or manager wants to know that a work environment they are responsible for has negatively impacted an employee's wellbeing. We are in business to create a great life for ourselves, our employees and the people we serve. We aren't in the business of damaging lives. Creating a Homeforce has the potential to give people the flexibility they desire to live life on their own terms. However, as mentioned at the beginning of this book, not all people are suited to working remotely. Even those who are may still need a better work connection than simply receiving an email every Monday with their tasks for the week.

An understanding of the sense of isolation an employee can feel when working from home, even when they are part of a larger team who may also be working from home, is a big consideration when creating a Homeforce. You need to consider how you as an employer can create a feeling of connectedness among your staff no matter where they are physically. There needs to be a regular pattern of connection.

So how can we make sure our team are building those necessary relationships when we aren't sitting next to each other, sharing birthday morning teas or impromptu lunch dates? And how do we stop the feelings of FOMO (fear of missing out) and loneliness when remote workers are comparing themselves to those in the office who are still doing those things? What do you do if all of your senior staff – all the managers – are choosing to come into the office five days a week, and more and more of the other staff start to do the same? When those staff who are 'present' start to be given all the good work, the opportunities and the praise? Feelings of disconnection and being left out will increase any sense of loneliness already being experienced.

But how do you do it? How do you replace the type of in-person communications that occur when people are in the same physical space? Or do you not need to?

**Maintaining boundaries**

On the flip side, trying to avoid feeling lonely can lead employees to always be 'on' and connected so they don't miss out. Enter the issue of maintaining effective boundaries.

When your office is in your home, or even worse at your dining room table, it can be hard to draw the line between work and home life. As you can see from the Swinburne study, concerns around blurred boundaries, distractions and trouble switching off are big challenges for remote workers. Other research has found that professionals work 25 extra minutes a day when remote, and managers an extra 14 minutes a day.[25] As a business owner or manager you might say that is your employees' problem and see it as a bonus for productivity. You might think it is up to them to learn how to separate when it's time to sit and attend to client work and when it's appropriate to do the laundry.

However, a lack of boundaries can have a negative effect on well-being. Some people really struggle to separate the different aspects and responsibilities in their life. When home is also work, all those work jobs are on your mind, and all the home jobs too, and all of a sudden it can feel very overwhelming. And we all know where that can end up. With a mental health issue.

> From my own experience, being a parent makes it even harder to maintain boundaries between work and rest of life when I'm working at home. There always seems to be something of my children's lying around that is driving me to distraction. Maybe it is an unmade bed, a pile of laundry, or that birthday invitation that needs a reply. As soon as I spot it, there's an internal struggle to stop work going out the window.
>
> For those of us with multiple demands on our time (like children or older parents), particularly in our home environment, it can be hard to add another set of demands - work demands - into the same space. It can feel like everything is competing.

---

25 NSW Innovation and Productivity Council 2020, NSW Remote Working Insights: Our experience during COVID-19 and what it means for the future of work, Council Research Paper, Sydney, 2020.

So how do employees put in place adequate boundaries, and what do we as business owners have to do with it? And why does it even matter?

All workers have a right to be disconnected from work – but how do you make sure that happens? As we said at the beginning of this chapter, you need to be prepared. It's important to understand the challenges that an employee might face in separating home and work and help them put strategies in place to draw those boundaries effectively.

For example, are there set working hours each day – similar to being in the office? Is it expected that work will be completed between 8 a.m. and 6 p.m.? What will you do if an employee is logging on at 9 p.m.? Or sending emails at 1 a.m.? Or working on weekends? Do you pat yourself on the back for having such conscientious employees who do what needs doing to get the work done? Or do you give them a call to let them know that working at those times isn't appropriate or desired?

The outcome of a call like that might be an employee who tells you that working after 7 p.m. when their children go to bed works for them. It's quiet, there are no distractions that seem to appear during the day, and they can focus. What do you do then?

There is no easy answer here. Part of creating a Homeforce, and finding people to join your Homeforce, is the opportunity for those people to work in a way that suits their lifestyle. The key is making sure that's exactly what is happening. That working those hours is actually desired by the employee as opposed to them feeling a sense of pressure, or simply being unable to switch off because the computer is just in the other room and they will just duck in and 'get a bit more done' to get a head start on tomorrow. As we all know – that is a fool's game.

And always keep in mind that, as a business owner or manager, the health of your employees is supremely important to the success of your business.

**Stop bullying**

It wouldn't be right to talk about mental safety at work without touching on bullying. Bullying in the workplace has become a widely recognised problem that can result in not just 'stop bullying' orders, workers compensation claims and prosecutions under safety laws, but also fundamental harm to company culture.

Bullying is not always easy to recognise, especially in a remote working arrangement. In one 'stop bullying' claim that was made in 2019–20 in the Fair Work Commission, the employee described events such as management not responding to his emails which he said 'excluded and isolated' him, and receiving a nasty email from his employer about taking stationery from the office, which he was using for work purposes.[26]

A distributed workforce will naturally result in more written communication. It is much easier to misread tone and intention, and may lead to jumping to conclusions. Managers need to be attuned to this possibility and have techniques in place to minimise any risks.

## CHALLENGE 5: PRIVACY AND SECURITY

When employees are in your office space, you have total control over the equipment they use, and where they are doing their work. They are using company-provided computers and other hardware, using software that you have obtained appropriate licences for, they are connected via a system network and using the company's internet connection. Any printed documents, like client information or staff procedure manuals, are kept in their allocated spaces and possibly in locked drawers, or at least behind doors which you have the ability to lock each night. All of these factors bring a sense of safety and security over your business. When there is so much uncertainty and

---

26  *Bailey v PCL Finance Pty Ltd; Illawarra Home Loans Pty Ltd T/A Illawarra Home Loans* [2020] FWC 3771.

insecurity around business it is a good feeling to get some wherever you can.

However, when you create a Homeforce you naturally lose some of these factors that previously might have made you feel safe. You no longer control the internet connection being used, can't so readily limit what staff are doing from their computers, and may not even own the computer they are using. You don't know where they are reading printed material, or leaving it lying around. Are they locking it away each night?

There are two things at play here:

- The need to feel in control. This comes back to your mindset, which we discussed at the beginning of this chapter. You need to be able to move beyond the fear mindset that having people working away from the office is going to cause damage to your business.

- A need to understand what is truly important to control. What are the actual risks from a privacy and security point of view, and what can you practically do to limit them?

### Computer and other hardware security

A risk that is often talked about is cyber-security. How do we stop third parties from hacking into employee personal computers at home? Is that even a risk? Yes – it is.

There are plenty of blogs on the internet telling of fixes to software to stop people being able to hack in – including to take over your webcam to spy on your activities. Those people (like me) who have tape over their cameras aren't just paranoid. But computer risks aren't just about the faceless predator out there somewhere surfing the web. Often risks are caused by the user's lack of knowledge.

For example, have we effectively trained staff in the risks of using free internet when out and about and quickly checking their emails on their phone? Do we even want to allow email access on phones?

That brings us to thinking about phones in general. If employees working from home need to be contacted that may naturally occur via phone. Is the employee using their house phone or mobile phone? Do other people in the house have access to that phone?

Maybe the answer is to provide computers and phones to all staff working from home. But is that financially viable for you? Or do we just need to provide separate internet connections and anti-virus software?

## Less obvious security and privacy risks

While all business owners will usually turn their mind to considering cyber-security risks to some degree, there are some other less obvious security and privacy risks that don't get the same kind of attention.

Picture this. An employee, Maddy, is working from home in her office. It's a separate room off the lounge room with its own lockable door which she locks each day when the working day is done. Maddy is a visual worker so tends to have a whiteboard full of information about the current work projects, drawings tacked up on the walls, and piles of paperwork spread around the room.

One day Maddy's partner is home sick and quietly relaxing on the lounge watching TV. At one point he gets up and makes himself a cup of coffee and decides to take one into Maddy and put it on her desk. He doesn't normally go in there because the door is locked so he takes a curious look around to see what's changed and notices some writing on the whiteboard.

Maddy takes a lot of calls during the day and can get quite animated. She leaves her office door open during the day to stop from feeling claustrophobic. Maddy totally forgets that her partner is home, takes a call and starts talking loudly about the latest takeover deal that her employer is planning. She later gets quizzed all about it by her partner, and has to awkwardly deflect all the questions and get him to promise not to say a thing about the juicy news he overheard.

How can you know as an employer that your employee isn't having a sensitive phone conversation in front of someone else? How do you know that private documents aren't being left in places where others can see and read them?

In Maddy's situation there are clearly lots of safeguards in place and yet there are still risks. What about the employee who is working from the dining room table and has a friend drop around for morning tea? How does that employee provide for security of documents and computer devices?

What about the employee who is a huge proponent of working from home and likes to post photos of their home office on social media? The #workingfromhome hashtag certainly grew in use exponentially in 2020. Do those photos pose a security risk – having the world know that there is a home office with confidential information in it? Perhaps accidentally sharing an image of a computer screen with something you didn't want known? Or more likely – the risk that someone zooms in on your photo to read what you've written on your whiteboard.

Breaching privacy and security laws has the potential to lead to big legal sanctions. Everything from fines to criminal prosecution. Often even worse – reputational damage, loss of clients and revenue.

## CHALLENGE 6: WORKING RELATIONSHIPS AND COLLABORATION

When we work in a team a core element of success is the relationships we develop. Your team members don't need to be your best friends − you just need to be able to work well together towards a common purpose. This can be more difficult in a remote working arrangement.

In the 2020 'NSW Remote Working Insights' report the second biggest barrier to success in remote work for the 1500 people surveyed was difficulty collaborating. Many also stated their working relationships and on-the-job learning were negatively impacted.

You would be hard pressed to argue that people act the same way in online video meetings as they do in person. The inability to interject in a conversation as easily, the difficulty in seeing when someone is ready to speak in a large group and similar challenges all leave people acting a bit less spontaneously and naturally. Unfortunately, this can lead to a reduced quality of collaborative conversation which may impact productivity. However, maybe this isn't such a great challenge for you. Ask yourself, how important is collaboration for any particular job in your business? Maybe it is more important that people get significant amounts of time to work undisturbed.

We've already explored earlier that poor relationships can lead to a negative effect on mental health. But there is more to it than that. Poor relationships negatively affect productivity. Also, in recent research, Michael McNamara found that the strength of a relationship between supervisor and staff member is the key factor when assessing the effectiveness of a supervision arrangement.[27]

So why does a remote relationship create such a challenge to relationships? It primarily comes down to one thing. Trust. Or more

---

27 *Supervision in the Legal Profession* (2020).

specifically – a lack of it. According to Patrick Lencione, the basis of all team dysfunctions is a lack of trust between team members.[28] If you can't be open with your team, it makes it hard to be an effective team member.

When people aren't in your immediate vicinity, there is often a feeling of having lost control. Like as a parent – when you turn around and your child isn't right behind you where they were two minutes ago before you got distracted bumping into a friend in the supermarket. You freak out, imagining kidnappings and all sorts of things, until you spot them calmly looking at something at the opposite end of the aisle from you. This is the sort of out-of-control feeling supervisors can have managing remote teams when they don't have trust in them.

Studies have shown that remote workers tend to do less small talking and socialising, which leads to lower levels of trust. This then leads to less collaboration and less innovation, which ultimately impacts overall business performance.[29]

Who's ever heard the comment: 'But how will I know if they are working if I can't see them?' I hear this all the time. Maybe you've even said this yourself. This is the often unspoken fear of a business owner or manager who receives a working from home request. It goes back to the mindset of the employer (or manager) and how they will manage a distributed workforce. As mentioned earlier – it can also be the fear of a peer who doesn't want to have to do more than their fair share.

A lack of trust can lead to micromanagement and expecting 24/7 availability from employees. So while some employees are always 'on' to combat loneliness, others sense this lack of trust from managers and teammates and feel like they always need to be 'on' to prove themselves.

---

28  *The Five Dysfunctions of a Team* (2012).

29  *Harvard Business Review*, 'Implications of Working Without an Office'.

This always being 'on' increases work pressure, stress and anxiety.[30] And so we cycle back around to poor mental health again and its negative impact on productivity.

We need to make sure a manager's style doesn't take away from all the positives which have come from giving employees the autonomy to choose where they work. It runs the risk of becoming a situation where we give with the right hand and take away with the left.

However, there is more to it than that. It's not just how managers feel about their team, it's how they like to manage. With a distributed team, many managers will need to adjust how they supervise and manage their staff. If you are the kind of manager who likes to 'walk the floors' to see whether someone is at their desk working, or likes to have an open-door policy and encourages people to regularly drop in with questions, or regularly takes staff members out for coffee to have a catch up, how are those practices going to translate when you aren't physically sharing the same space? How can you support your managers to transition to managing remote teams? Even more difficult – hybrid teams?

Gallup research found that remote worker engagement critically depends on one role – the manager.[31] It is crucial that you have the right managers as they are the key drivers of employee engagement and performance. Quality of a manager can account for 70% of the variance in team engagement.[32]

So how can we help build rapport between team members to enable successful supervision and collaboration? Obviously if people have worked together in person before a working from home arrangement starts, they are miles ahead. But what of a new hire? Someone who has never had the opportunity to work with their

---

30 *Harvard Business Review*, 'Remote Managers are Having Trust Issues'.

31 Gallup, 'How to Build Trust and Boost Productivity Within Remote Teams'.

32 Gallup, '8 Behaviours of the World's Best Managers'.

team in person? Consistent methods and training of managers will be an essential tool in managing your Homeforce.

## CHALLENGE 7: LEGAL BARRIERS

Quite a few of the challenges already discussed have some links to legal issues when running a remote workforce. For example, obligations to protect physical and mental safety, and obligations to protect confidential and private information of employees and clients.

Another consideration is compliance with applicable legislation, awards and enterprise agreements relating to employment conditions.

One of the big questions around distributed work teams is whether the working hours will remain synchronous (all working at the same time) or become asynchronous. However, if your employee is covered by an industrial award or agreement there might be obligations to pay overtime or penalty rates of pay when employees are working outside the typical hours of 6 a.m. to 6 p.m. Monday to Friday. But I hear you saying, the employee wants to work from 7 p.m. till 12 p.m. each night. In fact, they prefer to do so rather than working during daytime hours. Many employees are very keen to explore a remote arrangement which allows them to be unconstrained by typical working hours to better suit their life – true outcome-based work unconstrained by traditional concepts of working hours.

Have you heard the expression 'wage theft'? It's been bandied around a lot in the last couple of years, and it's a term which has embarrassingly attached itself to the actions of some big corporates like Woolworths, Coles, Target and Bunnings. You don't want this to happen to you.

Having an employee want to work outside the legally allowed spread of ordinary hours doesn't absolve you of the legal obligation to pay in accordance with the overtime requirements in an award. This usually results in rates of pay double the usual rate. So in the blink of an eye you have doubled your labour costs. If you don't comply you are exposing your company to prosecution and potential penalties of over \$60,000 per breach, not to mention backpay, and the risk of prosecution against you individually.

Some flexibilities were inserted into awards to deal with the pandemic, such as extensions to the spread of ordinary hours in the Clerks Private Sector Award 2020. But these flexibilities all have an end date and there is no guarantee of what will come next.

While it has been predicted that the future of work will include greater flexibility around when employees are expected (or allowed) to work,[33] we aren't there yet. So allowing staff to work outside normal permitted working hours does expose your business to potential risk in the present.

So you need to ask yourself – does the hourly rate or salary you are paying equate to at least what the employee would be entitled to under the award? Does the contract of employment legally vary the award in order to allow you to pay other than strictly in accordance with the award? Have you adequately protected yourself from a prosecution for breaching the award?

Another legal question that comes up regularly is whether it is okay to use some kind of surveillance over remote workers; for example, video surveillance or keystroke monitoring. Not only do we have overarching privacy laws, but we also have different surveillance rules in each state and territory. To avoid completely destroying any trust you might have with your remote workers and breaching any laws while you are at it, it's important to carefully

---

33 '9 Trends That Will Shape Work in 2021 and Beyond', Brian Kopp, 14 January 2021, *Harvard Business Review* (hbr.org/2021/01/9-trends-that-will-shape-work-in-2021-and-beyond?utm_medium=email&utm_source=newsletter_weekly&utm_campaign=insider_activesubs&utm_content=signinnudge&deliveryName=DM115785).

consider what kind of surveillance is appropriate and implement it correctly.

* * *

You as the business owner or manager need to understand your legal obligations to staff. You need to provide a safe place of work, watch out for their mental health and ensure you are meeting pay requirements. Once you're aware of your responsibilities you will be better prepared to have a conversation with your employee to negotiate the best working arrangement for you both.

## CONCLUSION

Now if you've read all of those challenges in one sitting you are probably feeling like there is nothing else to say. The challenges are insurmountable. Let's all go back to the office.

This is definitely not the case.

First, let me remind you that the title of this book isn't *The Seven Reasons Why You Should Never Allow Staff to Work From Home*. No – it's building a Homeforce to create an engaged and connected home-based team.

Second, remember the very first challenge? Let me remind you. It's your mindset. You as the business owner or manager (or both) will always run up against challenges – you face them every day running a business. Implementing a Homeforce is no different to any other project that you decide to tackle. The purpose of running through the challenges is so that they don't come as a surprise later and rock your confidence when you least need it.

Third, if you need reminding, go back and skim read all the

benefits of a distributed workforce. In my view, they more than counter the challenges.

The remainder of this book is focused on the 'how to' of creating an effective Homeforce in your business. As you go through and implement the 6-step strategy, any time a challenge rears up you will be able to move through it easier for having known about it in advance, and having the right mindset to tackle it.

So – let's get cracking!

# PART II

# The 6-step REMOTE Framework for Homeforce success

Creating an effective distributed team is not going to be easy. You've just read through the challenges. You know this is going to be a major change initiative for your business. The default central office model has been in place for a long time now and the diehards are all too ready to tell you that you just can't replace it. No matter how much time your team members have spent working remotely, embedding it as 'normal' is a separate thing all together.

For any change initiative to succeed you need time and dedication, especially for a big project like this one. But all the dedication in the world won't get you there if you don't have a good plan. If you're anything like me, the thought of creating a plan for a large project can feel overwhelming, so I've created a framework with the essential items for you.

Here are the steps in the Homeforce 6-step REMOTE Framework:

1. **R**emember your vision.

2. **E**stablish each role.

3. **M**anage the details.

4. **O**rganise your team.

5. **T**raining and support.

6. **E**valuate the result.

Following this process, and customising it to your particular circumstances, will give you the best chance to create and embed a distributed workforce in your business.

# CHAPTER 4

# Step 1: Remember your vision

'Stay true to yourself and your vision. Don't let any one person's opinion move you; listen, but be confident.'

Amanda Kahlow

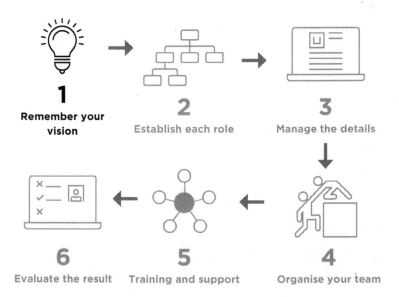

**1**
**Remember your vision**

**2**
Establish each role

**3**
Manage the details

**6**
Evaluate the result

**5**
Training and support

**4**
Organise your team

## YOUR VISION

When I first started my business, my only vision was having a business which would allow me the flexibility to work when and where I wanted. That vision wasn't big enough. It didn't look far enough into the future or give me a sense of direction for how I was going to grow the business and how it would positively impact my life and the lives of those I would ultimately work with and for.

You need a vision. A dream of the future you are trying to create.

Maybe you feel like you are too practical for visions. Does it sound a bit too much like a fortune teller or tarot reader? Aside from a brief blip when I was a teenager reading my astrology sign in the latest magazine, I've never been too keen on that kind of vision either.

But a business vision is different.

It involves imagining yourself in the place where you want your business to end up. It is a source of inspiration, to you and your team, to help you reach your goals. It is powerful to see yourself and how your business and world will look once the vision is achieved, and the research supports the power of visioning, too.

So don't stop at simply saying something like, 'My latest goal is to create a Homeforce where all staff are working from home all the time.' You need to delve deeper than that. Ask yourself what the future looks like for you, your employees, your clients and suppliers. How does the office look? Or maybe there isn't one. Has your business service model changed? There are so many things to consider.

## YOUR *WHY*

In a little while I'm going to take you through an exercise to create your own vision. You will be asked to answer these questions and more to help you visualise your future. But before we start the visioning exercise, let's take a step back.

Start with this question: why are you reading this book?

Why do you want to create a Homeforce? Go back to the beginning of this book and flick through the list of benefits. Which of them spoke to you most?

You might feel sick of hearing about the importance of knowing your *why*. It's been around for a long time in one form or another – the whole concept has been on everyone's lips, gained massive popularity and been part of most business talks in some form or another since Simon Sinek published his book *Start With Why* and did his famous TED Talk.

You might be sick of it, but it's popular for a good reason. Having a clear *why* or purpose in life is being touted as beneficial in personal lives and business. Individually, it has been found to lead to better mental and physical health. For organisations, purpose inspires. A PWC survey found that more than 90% of companies with a well-defined purpose delivered growth and profits at or above the industry average.[34]

It's easy when undertaking a big change project, like creating a distributed team, to get lost along the way. Once you start, everyone has an opinion. What you should do, or shouldn't do, what technology is best, what jobs definitely can't be done from home. Any and every aspect of the process has the potential to lead to debate.

That's why it is so important to know your *why*. Only by knowing this can you hold true to your vision and avoid getting caught up in someone else's view of what is right and wrong. You will be able to create your Homeforce your way, not someone else's.

In my case, my business started with just me as a solo entrepreneur working from home. I started my business at home because I wanted to save money, save time on travel and have more flexibility to participate in my children's lives. My first hire fell into my lap: another lawyer I knew who was dissatisfied in her current role and was looking for what I had. All of a sudden I had my vision: a Homeforce of mums (and maybe some dads) who wanted a flexible work life that gave them both a satisfying career and fulfilling home life.

---

34 hbr.org/2019/11/why-are-we-here.

I've broadened the vision since then, both for my team and the clients we serve, but that first vision was the start of my business really taking off.

Whenever I get tempted by nice office premises or my confidence is battered by people saying, 'You don't have an office?', I just refocus and remember my *why* for having a Homeforce in the first place.

A little warning here. If you start thinking about this and the only answer you can come up with is something like 'everyone else is doing it,' or even worse, 'I have to do it or we will go out of business,' you might want to stop and rethink your plans.

'Everyone else is doing it' has never been a good reason. I seem to have started repeating that advice a lot since my children reached primary school. But the same applies in the workplace. You need to have a strong belief in what you are doing for it to truly work.

Also, fingers crossed, massive workplace changes brought on by things like the coronavirus pandemic won't always be with us. So if you are just doing it to stop yourself going out of business while there are restrictions around access to workplaces then you need to look at this as a short-term plan. This framework is designed to help you create an ongoing distributed team – not a temporary one.

## CREATING YOUR HOMEFORCE VISION

There are lots of different ways to create a vision for the future, if you don't have one already. Following is an exercise I've created for you to give you some guidance. I've listed a few options to cater for different ways of thinking – feel free to change it up any way that works for you.

This is supposed to be fun. There is no right or wrong answer. Just let your own vision come.

## Step 1: Set aside the time

Give yourself the mental space and time required. A detailed vision won't just come about and take shape in the moments you have between other work tasks. As a leader there is always something demanding your attention. But creating a distributed team is not like any other project you will have undertaken. Take the time you need to make it happen.

That also means that blocking out one hour between two other meetings isn't going to cut it.

## Step 2: Choose a place free of distractions

As well as finding the time you also need to find the place. I suggest you find a place where you feel like you can daydream. No, your office is not likely to be that place. Having said that – if you have an office that is tidy, perhaps has a comfy chair, a calm feel, you won't be distracted by your emails or anyone walking in, and most importantly it lets you feel creative, then sure, give it a go.

Your office isn't like that? Mine either. Let's try somewhere completely different.

Maybe on the sand at the beach, or in a busy café with lots of noise and energy. Or perhaps you're like me and dream of a weekend away, free from work, kids and all the demands that go with it so that you can focus on truly relaxing. The perfect opportunity to vision your future.

Pick somewhere that resonates with you and make sure you've allocated the right amount of time to sink in and enjoy it.

## Step 3: Get your supplies

When you've worked out the time and place logistics you need to gather your supplies. If you are anything like me, I suggest you have lots of coloured pens and textas, a journal with a cover that speaks to you, some large butcher paper or A3 paper, some old magazines (with scissors and glue) and any other craft-like supplies you might have lying around or choose to buy for the occasion.

I can hear some of you moaning (or perhaps scoffing) as you read the word 'craft'. But trust me: visioning is all about getting creative. It can be really hard to be and feel creative when you are working on lined paper with a blue pen. Give colour a try.

The reason I suggested bringing along all of those different kinds of supplies is because we all think differently, and all create differently. Some of you will be naturally attracted to a fresh journal and a bright-coloured pen. Others will prepare to grab the big piece of butcher paper and start with textas.

For those of you who love your lined paper and blue and red pens – take those too. It doesn't really matter what you use – just that you do it.

### Step 4: Create your vision

Now it's time to start dreaming of the business and life you want for your future. Because we are all different in how we create, I've given you a few options to choose from; a mindmap, a vision story and a vision board. You might stop at one, or take the time to do all three. Whatever works for you.

### Mindmap

Whatever your ultimate tool of choice I suggest you start off your vision with a mindmap. A mindmap is a diagram that helps you visually organise information. The central idea of your mindmap is HOMEFORCE. Write it big and bold in the middle of your page. Write your *why* down there too to keep it front and centre. From there you add branches of all the different thoughts that occur to you. (Can you see why I suggested the butcher paper?) Remember – you aren't creating an action plan here. You are imagining what your business is going to look like when you've created the Homeforce of your dreams.

Here's an example of a mindmap.

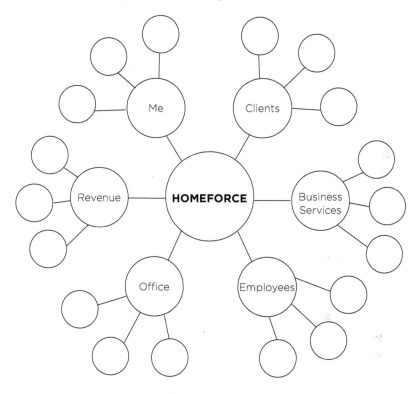

To give you some inspiration, I've created a list of questions for you:

- **What does it look like having a business with a distributed team?** Where are they all working? At home? In regional or suburban hubs? Co-working spaces? How does your central office look now? Is there one at all? If yes, are people hot desking from time to time? Is it a large, open-plan space? How do people interact in that space? Has there been financial growth as a result of increased productivity from employees?

- **What about your clients?** How are you serving them? Have you created a point of difference with your service by providing a travel-to-you service? Or perhaps your point of difference is that you have gone completely online in all service provision. Is your reputation for innovative service delivery leading to increased sales?

- **How about your employees?** Is turnover down? Do you have a larger number of employees? Are they scattered around the world? Are they working from computers and using other office equipment that you own and supplied? How are you paying them? Have you made financial savings because you don't need to pay the big salaries to attract the right kind of staff? How are you all staying in touch? Do you have a yearly retreat where staff get together from around the world? Or perhaps quarterly if you are closer?

- **Let's not forget about you.** How are you working now? Are you dedicating fewer hours to work than before? Maybe less time commuting, 'getting ready' or engaging in work-related things that you don't need to be part of? Are you happier than before? What is it about your new way of working that is making you happiest?

Ask yourself those questions (close your eyes if you dare) and picture yourself in the future. Start noting down your thoughts. Use different-coloured pens for different branches, highlight your keywords, and don't be afraid to get messy. There's no prizes for neat and tidy in this exercise.

## Vision story

A completed mindmap may be enough for you to feel ready to tackle the next steps in the framework. However, if you have the time and the inclination then think about writing out your vision story. This might even feel more natural than drawing a mindmap for those of you who like to work in sentences.

A vision story is written in the present tense – where you see yourself at a point in the future. Most people suggest projecting five or ten years in the future, however I think with the vision of a Homeforce you could make it either three or five years. Use whatever you think is a realistic timeframe to have your Homeforce created, embedded and having a real impact on your business.

Your vision story should be in powerful, positive language. Let those earlier questions and your mindmap guide you, and write about the current state of play. Be positive, yet don't ignore the challenges that you've overcome or perhaps the unwanted effects such as losing certain clients or employees along the way. Don't be future looking – it is all about the here and now: what have you achieved, and a straightforward statement about what still may need to be done. It also needs to be really specific. The more specific you are, the easier it will be to measure success.

If you're feeling a little unsure, then take a look at this sample vision story I've created.

**7 June 2024**

The WHO has finally called an end to the coronavirus COVID-19 pandemic. The world has returned to normal. We can visit other countries again, quarantining is a thing of the past and lockdowns are a distant memory.

What isn't a memory is working from home.

We now have 90% of our team working from home at least three days each week. There is no set requirement on the number of hours they need to be in the office, and most people only come in for scheduled meetings that are required to be face to face. There aren't too many of them because we've been able to get clear on which meetings are truly for collaboration purposes and which are just for conveying information.

When they do come in, collaboration is a joy. The meeting rooms are beautifully designed to promote creativity, and there are lots of little places to encourage break-out conversations. There are open-plan workstations and offices too – as not everyone likes to be in a shared open space.

Most of our new recruits now come from internal referrals as everyone is happy to promote our business as a great place to work. Workplace disputes and complaints are at an all-time low and we've even won an award for 'Best Wellbeing at Work'!

It's a condition of employment that everyone has a home office set up, including their own computer. We provide home internet and security and all the best software tools to allow team members to excel from home. The first week of employment is in the central office (we even fly them in if they don't live locally) where they undergo a rigorous induction program to ensure they understand our business and – importantly – how to operate in a distributed team. Then they are able to choose where they work each day by making arrangements with their manager and their team.

The transition hasn't been all roses. We lost some team members who preferred being in the office 100% of the time, or who couldn't learn to manage their teams effectively when they were in distributed locations. We lost some clients too. But we gained a lot more!

How? Because those happy employees are so much more productive. Our clients love how responsive our team members are, that they are not paying us to maintain fancy CBD office premises, and that we are truly walking the talk when it comes to building a team culture that is beneficial for the employees and our business.

Overall, we have reduced our costs by 30% (mainly due to only needing a much smaller office space) and our revenue is up by a whopping 50%.

## Vision board

Another option is to create a vision board. This is for the really creative types and visual thinkers. Take the key thoughts from your mindmap and find pictures that best show those ideas in visual format. Print out some photos that represent your vision and stick them on. Maybe it's an employee working at home with a child in the background, or an office space that is all open plan and set up for hot desking. Choose some keywords and quotes and put them on your vision board too. Choose whatever resonates with you.

For some people it really helps to have a visual reminder of what they're aiming for. If this is you – think about making a vision board you'd be pleased to hang in your office. Pretty it up! Use colourful pens, and find items that add texture. You'll end up with something that was fun to create, looks good and can inspire you everyday.

If cutting up magazines or printing photos isn't for you – then you could try a digital vision board. Same concept as I've described above, however in this version you are just locating pictures and words online and adding them to a digital page. Canva is an incredible design tool which would be great for this. The finished product makes a great desktop background.

\* \* \*

Whatever you have created that most speaks to you – mindmap, vision board, vision story – you need to hold that front and centre while you go on the Homeforce journey. Put it on the wall, on your desk, or wherever is most likely to keep you inspired.

## THE ROLE OF THE LEADER

### Commit to change

People generally don't like change. It activates the amygdala and creates the freeze, fight or flight response. You will have people on your team jumping for joy and begging to help. The early adopters. You will have others who actively resist – throwing up all sorts of questions and emphasising challenges. The naysayers. Then others will just freeze – eyes wide open, carefully watching to see which side will prevail. The watchers.

I've said it a couple of times already, but it's worth repeating. Creating, embedding and managing a distributed team is a *change* process. What I haven't maybe emphasised enough yet is that you are going to be the leader in this change process.

You need to get comfortable with that.

Change is not easy. As the leader (or one of them), you need to be prepared for all the reactions. You need to stay committed and not wobble at the first signs of pushback or difficulty. This is where your visioning becomes so important. Creating a beautiful vision and putting it on your wall isn't enough.

For a vision to become reality you need to be committed to achieving it. The only way to achieve it successfully is to bring your team and clients along for the ride. You need to get their buy in right from the beginning, and this means sharing and communicating your vision.

By taking the time to create a proper vision of the future you can describe it to your team in a way that allows them to see it. They can see what it will look like for the business as a whole and their place in it. They will be able to add their own vision to yours of how the Homeforce will impact their lives. Their commitment, along with your own, is what will make the change happen successfully.

One great big benefit you have is that your team and management have already had the experience of distributed work – pretty much the whole world has as a result of the pandemic. You can use those experiences to anchor your vision in their reality.

Back in early 2019, RSM Australia (a large accounting and consulting business) already had a flexible work policy. However they were keen to embed this further in the business by educating the senior leadership group on managing flex work successfully. When we started working with them, we initiated a Flexible Work Education session with the Perth office (and later did the same in Melbourne). In these group sessions with senior leaders, there were some concerns around the impact that flex work would have on productivity, engagement and culture. All valid concerns. To help overcome those concerns during these sessions we worked with the senior leadership team to anchor the benefits of flexible work in their minds, and workshopped potential solutions to the challenges that were identified. An essential part of this was having leaders identify 'success' stories from within RSM of people who were already working flexibly and remotely and doing so with positive results for themselves and RSM. This made it a lot easier to overcome any suggestion that 'remote working' only works for other companies. RSM were lucky. These actions, and initiatives that were taken afterwards, provided the right degree of groundwork just in time for the massive changes that hit the world of work in 2020.

As I understand it, RSM continued on this journey by reviewing their previous flexible work offerings since the COVID-19 pandemic. The People & Culture Team undertook a massive consultation process with all Partners, Office Managing Partners, the Executive, and staff and now offers Flex@RSM 2.0. A take two and enhancement of previous arrangements, where now flexible work is about changing the way they think about where, when and how work is being done. I'm pleased to say RSM have made the transition to a more flexible working model and it's having a positive impact on the business.

## GET GOOD AT COMMUNICATING

If you were paying close attention, you probably noticed a common theme among all the challenges set out in the previous chapter. Did you spot it? Yep – communication issues. That's why you will also notice the same common theme in all of the REMOTE steps.

After 20 years of being an employment lawyer and working with many hundreds of clients providing advice on people problems – the underlying factor contributing to most issues is a lack of communication.

People like to know where they stand. They need to know what is expected of them. They need to be able to effectively communicate what they expect of others. This goes both ways. It's the same in any relationship – but I find people are particularly unforgiving of communication issues in the workplace.

A failure to effectively communicate expectations leads to a mismatch which ultimately creates conflict. Unfortunately, if that conflict isn't resolved early enough the wrong behaviours become normalised until such a time as someone can't take it anymore and the relationship breaks down completely.

Each of the six steps in the REMOTE Framework is going to require you to engage in effective communication. Communicating the vision is only the beginning. You will need both internal and external communication plans to cover all of your various stakeholders all along the way. Employees need to know how it affects them as individuals and the team they work within, clients want to know whether they will still receive the same level of service, and suppliers want to know who's going to be at the office when they drop off office supplies or other equipment – or if an office will even still exist.

So, as you go through each step keep note of where you need good communication. Think about what you will need to say, who you need to say it to, when, who you need to listen to, remember your *why*, and then work out how you can communicate effectively.

## BE PREPARED TO CHANGE

It is very rare for visions to come out exactly as you image them. This is normal. Things change along the way and it is important that you allow yourself to adapt.

For example, a lot of businesses are coming out with statements about their policies to allow distributed work after the pandemic restrictions are lifted. In the legal industry, it's been pretty common to see statements from large CBD-based national firms saying they will be implementing a 60:40 model – with three days in the office and up to two elsewhere.

The rationale for this has included things like the need to facilitate contact, and that it's important for the culture and make up of the firm. It's not clear how much of these policies are based on employee wishes. Other businesses are surveying their staff. For example, HSBC surveyed about 33,000 staff based in Hong Kong and found 25% wanted to work from home full time, 25% wanted to work in the office full time, and the remaining half wanted a hybrid arrangement. So HSBC created three options: primarily work from home (four days at home), primarily office (up to two days at home) and full-time office.[35]

---

35  Grace Dean, Business Insider Australia, 18 November 2020.

This shows the importance of finding out where your people are. Ask for their help. Create plans together using the next steps of the REMOTE Framework. Find out what your employees like and don't like. How much resistance is there? Is there willingness to change? To upskill? It doesn't mean they will get exactly what they want, or that it won't change (change is actually guaranteed) but it's always good to know where you're starting from and to take the pulse as you move along.

Repeat the vision (or its updated version) often. Share progress updates in regular team meetings. Share success stories — those of your business and others. Let your team hold you accountable to do the work. Only by standing strong in your vision and being willing to constantly restate it will you be able to create the Homeforce you desire.

---

## Step 1 summary

Answer the question: 'Why do I want to create a Homeforce?'

Create your vision of a Homeforce using the four-step process:

- Set aside the time.
- Choose a place free of distractions.
- Organise your supplies (the more colourful the better in my book).
- Craft your vision whatever way suits you.

Share your vision with your team.

Understand your role as the leader of change in this process.

---

CHAPTER 5

# Step 2: Establish each role

'You can't really know where you are going until you know where you have been.'

Maya Angelou

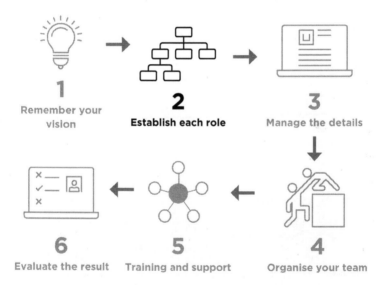

**WHERE ARE YOU NOW?**

You should be feeling pretty great right now, riding high on the vision of what your future can hold if you stick to the plan. Now it's time to truly get stuck into the work. Let's start by working out where you are right now to see how far you need to go to reach that beautiful vision. This means giving your organisational structure a full appraisal.

Now the fact is that you wouldn't have even picked up this book if you didn't believe that at least some of the roles in your business could be worked from home. In fact – most of you have probably seen this happening if you were forced to start moving staff to work from home during the pandemic. But this step in the framework asks you to go beyond the obvious and dig a little deeper. Look at how each role can be worked from home on a full-time basis, or regular part-time basis, rather than simply in case of emergency. Also – let's not forget those roles that you are dead set can't be worked from home. Let's challenge all those assumptions you might not even be aware you have.

The main goal here is to take a look at your organisational structure, the roles you have and how they work together, and how all of the business processes and operations function.

If you're game, don't stop there. Although it's generally outside the scope of this book, I also suggest you use the opportunity to take a look at your financial position, the clients you are working for, and the services you are providing. After you've implemented your Homeforce and had it running for a while there will be a review period. If part of your vision is to improve your financial position, it will be useful to have a true snapshot of that position now. So let's poke around in all the nooks and crannies and see what we come up with.

## MAPPING OUT THE ROLES IN YOUR BUSINESS

If you don't already have an organisational chart, get that butcher paper and the coloured textas back out of the cupboard and draw it out. We are not concerned about the individual people in the business at this stage – that comes later. What we want to know is what roles are being performed and how they relate to each other.

You might even draw in the aspirational roles you have in mind for when the business grows.

Now you've got the role titles sorted out, let's dig a little deeper. If you can, this is the perfect time to get your management team involved. For ease of reference, I'll keep referring to what 'you' need to do, but that 'you' could also be one of your managers – by all means, delegate appropriately.

We need to know what work is being done in each of those individual roles. The best place to start to figure this out is by talking to managers and pulling out the existing job descriptions. Don't have any? Don't worry. I've created a template job description and inserted a completed example below that you can use to guide you through the matters you need to consider so you can create them.

A word of warning: it's important to be clear on the purpose of a job description. A job description, or position description, also known as a JD or PD, is created for a specific role. It is *not* created for the person who happens to currently be in the role. So, although you might start by considering all the tasks being performed by the person currently in the role, this should not be the only thing guiding your review. For example, some people have extra skills so are given more tasks than you actually need in a role. Others have fewer skills, so tasks are removed. You need to consider how the role looks in the optimal scenario. What are the core functions and what are extra that are just related to the specific person?

## Do I really need job descriptions?

In my opinion – yes.

Aside from measuring the ability for a job to be done remotely, a job description has other uses. It helps you employ the right people, as you spend the time actually listing out what you need done and then use this as the basis for your job advertisement. Later it helps you guide a review of their performance in a measured way. You've clearly set out the expectations of the role and can have conversations about what is or isn't being done without fear of someone saying they didn't know what was expected. It is also important when you are assessing whether a person can perform the inherent requirements of their role. That's why it is so important to be honest and think carefully about the true requirements of a role and make sure they are properly communicated.

It's not unusual for me to have a client who has job descriptions but never looks at them. Or even more common – the client who blankly refuses to have them. Do you ever hear yourself saying, 'I don't want job descriptions because then I'll have employees telling me "I'm not doing that. It's not in my job description".'?

Don't get me wrong – there are absolutely employees who will give you that response. But there are ways around it. One is to include a general statement near the end of the task list in the job description that says, 'All other tasks as reasonably required of the position.' It's a nice catch all. If you start finding that you are having to rely on that statement rather a lot then it should tell you that you haven't properly articulated what that role requires – or that the role has started to morph into something different. Or worse – that you've hired the wrong person!

The second and much more valuable tip for avoiding the employee who has memorised each task on their job description, and won't do another thing, is creating a great culture with a focus on teamwork. It is most common to find the 'It's not in my job description' employee in an environment where everyone is focused on individual rewards rather than the outcome the team is trying to achieve. It's also more common where an individual employee has really low engagement in their job and the workplace. If that's the case – they probably aren't performing at the required level either and it's time for some performance improvement conversations.

## Writing a job description

If you've decided to shake off your concerns and give JDs a go, then it's useful to follow a template with all the essential sections set out for you. You can see a job description template I've created below. You can also download a copy here: 3dhrlegal.com.au/homeforce/resources.

### JOB DESCRIPTION – ADMINISTRATION OFFICER

| | |
|---|---|
| **Job Title:** | **Administration Officer** |
| **Job Type:** | **Full-time        Part-time        Casual** |
| **Limited Term:** | **[insert if applicable e.g. 6 months]** |
| **Location:** | **Perth [insert]** |
| **Reporting To:** | **[Insert position]** |

### Job Role

*[Insert a summary paragraph about the main purpose of the role.]*
The Administration Officer is responsible for the day-to-day task and administration management. The role requires multi-tasking across a broad range of responsibilities, including scheduling, communications management, file management and more general clerical duties.

### Main duties and accountabilities:

*[List the main duties and responsibilities here.]*
- Being the first point of contact for our clients
- Assisting with scheduling and managing the company diary
- Drafting task lists, monitoring progress and report summaries
- File management

- Managing incoming and outgoing documents, including scanning and electronically registering incoming mail and documents and sending mail
- Assisting our accountant with bookkeeping, invoices, disbursements and reimbursements
- Other clerical duties, as requested from time to time

### Selection Criteria and Capability Framework

| Competency | Essential | Desirable |
|---|---|---|
| Qualifications<br><br>[What qualifications will assist the person to do the role?] | | • *Diploma or Certificate IV in Business Administration*<br><br>• *University Qualifications* |
| Skills and Understanding<br><br>[What skills will be used daily?]<br><br>[List skills needed for the job, including any technical or interpersonal skills] | • *Intermediate to advanced Microsoft Office skills (Word, Excel, PowerPoint and Outlook)*<br><br>• *Excellent verbal and written communication*<br><br>• *Organised and able to meet deadlines* | |

| | | |
|---|---|---|
| Prior Experience<br><br>[What type and how much experience is needed] | • *2 years previous experience in a similar role/ industry* | • *Previous work in the professional services industry or in a remote working environment* |
| Behavioural Characteristics<br><br>[What are you looking for?] | • *Passion for the role*<br>• *Shared values*<br>• *Exceptional organizational skills*<br>• *Excellent written and verbal communication*<br>• *Have high standards and be driven to provide proactive assistance to resolve issues efficiently and assist other team members*<br>• *Able to work remotely* | • *Be keen to embrace new technology to enhance the delivery of the business' services* |
| Performance Goals<br><br>[The level of performance you expect from the employee] | • *Complete administration tasks on time*<br>• *Deal with clients, suppliers and other employees professionally at all times* | |

I've provided some explanations below of each of the sections in the job description template. To help you work through it, I've listed some questions to ask yourself, shared some examples and also made it clear what *doesn't* belong in a job description. What you don't put in can often be as important as what you do.

Also – don't forget that you are not the keeper of all knowledge. Once you've had an attempt at writing the job description it's time to turn it over to the person who is performing the role and their supervisor. Who knows better what actually happens during the day? You may be surprised to learn that a task has become redundant or has been moved to someone else's role. As we've already said – but keep saying because it's so important – creating a Homeforce is not an individual pursuit. You will need to bring the whole team along for the ride so it's best to involve them where you can.

## What to include in a job description

We start with the basic data – what is the role called? What senior role does this position report to? What are the minimum qualifications that someone needs to complete this role satisfactorily? For example – if recruiting for an engineer, do you require them to be a qualified engineer with a university degree? Or perhaps you don't care if they have a degree and are happy just knowing that they have, say, 10 years of experience in a similar role.

What about a homecare support worker serving clients in the aged care or disability sector? They will need a specific type of licence in order to drive the vehicle that your company owns and uses for transport of clients. It's not much good if they have the wrong licence. They will also need a Police Clearance, and perhaps a Working with Children check.

Once you have basic qualifications out of the way, move on to considering skills. For example, the engineer might need to be proficient in CAD design software, an administration assistant might need an expert level of Microsoft Office skills, a fast typing speed or knowledge of a specific phone system. It might be that some things are obvious in this section, yet you will likely come back here again after you've done the next section as more ideas come to you. Remember – just because you are writing something in this list doesn't mean you can't hire someone to fill this position who doesn't have that skill. You might decide that some skills can be taught on the job. What you are creating here is your ideal candidate.

Next – experience. Is there a certain number of years of on-the-job experience that you want a person in this position to have? Remember – this is not your job advertisement – this is your job description for the ideal candidate.

Now we move on to the actual tasks being performed by the employee. To make this easier – break it down into daily, weekly, monthly, quarterly and yearly tasks. You might not list them that way on the job description (although maybe that style will work well for you), but it will help you focus on the job tasks in a strategic way.

When writing each task, be specific. For example, fast typing speed becomes 'type at 90wpm (words per minute)'. Answer the phones becomes 'answer the phones quickly and courteously'.

Don't get too carried away though. Some information doesn't belong in a job description. Let's take a salesperson role for example. A salesperson is employed to sell products or services. However, the sales targets for the individual don't belong in the job description. The targets might differ based on years of experience, remuneration, commission rates and so on. So the job description provides for the generic task, and then you will have an individual performance plan with each salesperson.

Another great example is a receptionist role where the person is required to answer the phones. It's easy to get carried away and start thinking about how quickly you want them to answer the phone (no more than three rings), the words you want them to use, the voice tone to use, and how quickly messages are to be returned if you miss a call. However, if you are going to provide that much instruction around the procedure for answering the phones, it is necessary to consider whether that's actually what you need – a separate procedure document.

If it's getting a bit overwhelming, ask for some help. It can be really helpful to have another person – a team member or someone like me – to do a brainstorm and sharpen your answers by asking the right questions.

What you should be starting to see here is that a job description is just one of the documents that can be used to clarify the work done by an individual role. You can then have performance guidelines, processes and procedures for individual tasks, and a code of conduct (or 'house rules') setting out the general behaviour expected of an employee in your workforce. And let's not forget their contract of employment. Don't try to cram all of this into a job description or it will be completely overwhelming and end up in the drawer never to be seen again.

If you're aiming for a gold star then I'd recommend you create a job description for each role, make a list of anything that you think needs its own process or procedure document (the best person to create these is the person actually doing each task), and make plans to work on creating a code of conduct too (which ideally needs whole workforce input). The individual measures form part of Step 4 in the framework. Remember – don't skip over a role just because you don't think it can be worked from home. There is a possibility that some tasks can – even if it only equates to a day a week.

## ASSESSING EACH JOB TO WORK FROM HOME

You might have become deeply involved writing all of your job descriptions and mapping out how they all work together, so that you've forgotten why you started. Don't worry – I'm here to remind you. It's all about working out whether or not an individual role can be worked from outside the central office. You are testing the 'remote-ability' of all roles in the business.

Now – just because you've mapped out that a role has in-person touchpoints doesn't automatically rule it out of being able to be worked from home. This is when you can get creative and consider alternatives.

Let's take the receptionist role again. Traditionally a receptionist spent most of their time greeting customers and visitors and answering phones. There are still some workplaces where this remains true. But it is far less common than it used to be. These days a receptionist is usually an administration officer who is located at the reception desk so that they can also greet people who arrive at the office. In many workplaces it's not uncommon to find the reception desks empty with only a bell for visitors to ring. Sometimes a staff member simply has a line of sight from their desk to the reception to be able to see when visitors arrive.

So have a think about your reception role. How many times is that person actually greeting a visitor during a day? How many phone calls are received on the general office line – or do most clients and other people call direct lines of team members? How much face-to-face time with visitors actually occurs? If it's only a few people a day, perhaps having a reception desk unattended is not really that big a deal. If you don't know, set up a logbook to log the in-person activity at the reception desk.

When considering each role, it will be useful to have a discussion with the person who is currently performing the role. Remember the importance of involving the team? Well, here is another opportunity to do just that. Like you did with the job description, talk to the individual currently performing the role and point out the tasks that you feel may need to be done in an office environment, or face to face. Ask them to come up with alternative ways to complete the task. Remember it's not just you who is benefiting from having a distributed team – those individual team members will receive their own individual benefits. So if they are keen, they will help you find a way to make it work.

Again, this is going to be a great time to involve your wider team. For the receptionist to have the ability like others to work from home, they are going to need other team members to step up. You will need a culture of teamwork and cooperation to help make a Homeforce a win for everyone, not just the chosen few.

## Calculate a percentage

At the end of the assessment, you should be aiming to know how much of each job needs to be done in an office, and consider that on an overall weekly basis. Taking me in my role as a lawyer for example, I don't need to be in an office environment with any of my team members on a weekly basis. It may be the case that we choose to meet together from time to time, but in order to complete my tasks there is no business need for it on a regular basis. So the assessment for my role is 0% needed in the office.

You can see how the same reasoning can be applied to most knowledge worker jobs.

It becomes a little trickier when we are thinking about those people who take on roles like receptionist. You could of course simply say that you will no longer need that role at all if you create a complete distributed team, as there will be no office for customers or others to visit. Maybe you will move to a serviced office set up, if deliveries are needed often.

Alternatively, if that is a bit radical for you and you need or want to maintain your office premises, then is it possible for those face-to-face reception tasks to be shared among those who are present in the office on any given day? If you consider that possible, then similarly the assessment might be 0% need for the receptionist role to be in the office.

Once you've done this percentage assessment for each role, it's helpful to put all of the roles into one of four buckets. According to McKinsey research,[36] roles can be classified into four different categories based on the value moving a role to remote can deliver:

1. Fully remote (net positive value-creating outcome).

2. Hybrid remote (net neutral outcome).

3. Hybrid remote by exception (net negative outcome, but can be remote if needed).

4. On site (not eligible for remote).

Option 4 is for those jobs that just can't be worked remotely. For example, the on-site construction jobs, nursing in hospitals, delivery drivers and the like. For the remaining jobs you are considering whether the pros outweigh the cons, or vice versa, in having a job fully or partly remote. Remember — just because a role can be worked fully remote doesn't mean it has to be, and just because it's not ideal for a job to be remote (hybrid by exception) doesn't mean you have to put it in the on-site category. This is all about assessing the role — how it works with a particular individual is a whole separate question.

---

36 'Reimagining the Office and Worklife after COVID-19', June 2020.

## Step 2 summary

- Create an organisational chart.
- Create a diagram showing how each different role interacts with the others.
- Draft job descriptions for each role in the organisation.
- Give each job a percentage requirement for time in the office on a weekly basis.
- Highly recommended: conduct an overall business assessment (include financial position, products/services sold, clients worked for, strength of business processes, and so on) to provide a baseline for a later assessment of the benefits of the Homeforce.

CHAPTER 6

# Step 3: Manage the details

'There is no magic in magic. It's all in the details.'

Walt Disney

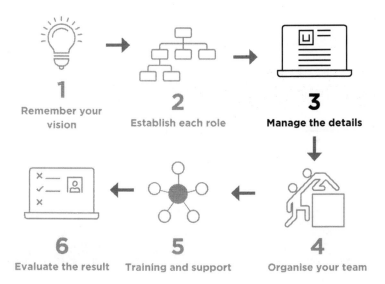

**CREATING YOUR HOMEFORCE POLICY**

Up to this point things have been very high-level. We've focused on your overall goals and vision and done an objective assessment of the business and the individual roles within it. Now it's time to examine how this is going to play out on an individual basis. It's time to manage the details.

Remember earlier in the book I wrote about how not all jobs are suitable to be worked from home, and not all people are either? Well – this is where you put that concept into practice. This step is designed to help you work out your minimum requirements for a distributed team, and to communicate them all in your Homeforce policy.

Whether you currently have a staff member in the office or are recruiting for a new job, if they are not going to be co-located with you there are special considerations that need to be met. These considerations are designed to ensure you maintain productivity and don't put your business at risk of a legal claim. The five essential areas that you need to cover in your policy are:

1. working at home safely

2. working at home productively

3. using appropriate tools and resources

4. implementing appropriate security measures

5. choosing appropriate insurance.

Nothing should feel new here. Each of these issues was discussed at the beginning of the book in the challenges of creating a Homeforce. This is your opportunity to address these challenges. Let's take them one at a time and work out how you will deal with them in your business.

Let's consider each of these five issues.

## 1. WORKING AT HOME SAFELY

Safety is often something that is completely overlooked or completely overdone. You can choose to rely totally on an employee's common sense and not address it at all – I mean, surely everyone knows it's not a good idea to lounge on your bed with a cup of hot coffee while working on your laptop? Or you can specify a whole list of safety instructions and require mandatory compliance assessments.

Where you find yourself on the scale will depend on a lot of factors, such as the type of industry you are in (for example, mining industry personnel have safety requirements hammered into them from early on), whether you've had safety issues in the past (for example, a staff member with RSI or back pain from poor ergonomics) and how much of a control freak you are.

## Self-assessments by staff

At a minimum I suggest that you require every employee working outside a central office to complete a self-assessment of their working environment. The self-assessment needs to specify the work location and assess its various parts. For example, does the employee have a proper chair? Does the employee have a desk to perform their work? Are these two pieces of equipment set up ergonomically to protect the employee from developing physical injuries?

What about the other areas of the house that the employee needs to use when at home – the kitchen and bathroom? Are these rooms safe? Are the passages between all of these rooms safe and free of hazards? Are there stairs? Are there noise issues? Safe Work Australia has some fantastic resources and guidelines about performing these kinds of assessments.[37] We also have a sample you can download at 3dhrlegal.com.au/homeforce/resources.

Importantly, the employee needs to sign off this assessment. If you are going to rely solely on a self-assessment then you want them to sign off that it is true and correct. You also need to ensure you

---

37  Go to www.safeworkaustralia.gov.au.

have a copy on file. That way, if something does go wrong at home and you find it was partly caused by something that the employee lied about on the assessment, you might be able to rely on that to reduce your liability in any legal claim.

Also – don't forget: if an employee is going to be working at any other location (such as a holiday house) then a separate assessment needs to be completed for each work location. It completely defeats the purpose of doing the assessment in the first place if the employee simply works wherever they want when they want.

One more thing. Reliance on a self-assessment is only good if it's kept up to date. Have some triggers in place for review. For example, an annual update and also a commitment from employees that they will notify you when they move house and need to do a new assessment.

If these assessments sound way too complicated, or you want to provide for greater flexibility like the desire to work at different cafés from time to time, an alternative is a shorter form assessment an employee can do at any location when they arrive there to work. It might have questions like: Have you checked the floor/area for trip hazards? Is the chair upright? Is the desk at a minimum height? It's kind of like creating a mini toolbox meeting an employee can have with themselves before commencing work.

**Home inspections**

Inspections can be a contentious issue. Probably not so much if the employee is working from a co-working space, but what if they are working from home? Requiring an employee to make their home available for an inspection sounds intrusive, and definitely doesn't feel like it fits with the culture of trust that you need to have for an effective Homeforce. If you strongly feel this way – then don't do one.

Often a good alternative, and one I recommend in any event is to require employees to provide photos of their working space.

There should also be a requirement to send in new photos any time something changes. For example, the employee buys a new desk or chair, or moves their workspace to another section of their home.

However, in your Homeforce policy I recommend giving yourself the right to request an inspection if for some reason you decide you need to. For example, what if you hear that an employee is doing substantial renovations to their home? How are they managing to work through the noise, the people coming and going, and the dust and the mess? What if their whole office has been gutted – where are they actually working now?

Of course, many of these questions can be answered through a simple conversation, and it may be that in times of disruption an employee simply returns to working from the office (if there is one), but again, having the right to inspect is still a good thing to keep up your sleeve.

If you are going to conduct a home inspection there are a few rules to follow:

- First, make sure you schedule it in advance. Just like a rent inspection, you need to give the employee time to tidy up their work area, put away the kids' toys and make sure there are no ants eating the crumbs left out in the kitchen. There is nothing to be gained from randomly knocking at your employee's door at 9:30 a.m. to catch them unaware. This isn't your chance to live out your dreams of being a private investigator.

- Second, don't take the home inspection as a right to walk through an employee's entire house and pass judgement. Stick to the areas that are deemed to be a workplace – the workstation, bathroom, kitchen and passages between. If all of these areas are safe there is nothing further to see.

- Third, if you are going to the trouble of conducting a home inspection you should have some kind of formal assessment to complete. If you are looking for something simple, just follow the self-assessment that the employee completed and use that as a guide to create a new checklist for a home inspection. Tick it off as you go and take the time to briefly discuss any issues before you leave. A quick discussion can resolve an issue a lot more easily than sending a formal report one week after the fact.

## Work hours v personal time

As discussed in the challenges section, managing employee safety also means knowing when they are working. We don't want employees working 24/7 and burning out. Also, when we are dealing with someone working at home, we need to know the boundaries for when something is a 'workplace' accident, versus just being an accident they have at home. For example, what if the employee uses the same computer for work and personal use? When they sit down at the desk in the evening to do some personal work and also happen to check work emails, and then twist their ankle standing up – is that a workplace accident? Or if they go for a run during the day and fall over – is that a workplace accident?

What about sex?

Believe it or not that was the question in a workers compensation claim that went all the way to the High Court of Australia.

A public servant was required to travel to country NSW for work. One evening in her work provided motel room, she was having sex when a light fitting dislodged and fell on her, injuring her nose and mouth and requiring hospital treatment. The claim was initially accepted by Comcare before being revoked, and finally reached the High Court after multiple appeals.

> The big question? Were the woman's injuries caused 'in the course of her employment'?
>
> The High Court said no - having sex wasn't in the course of her employment because the employer did not induce or encourage her to engage in the activity. It was not enough that the employer had induced or encouraged her to be at that motel.[38]

All of this points to a need to be able to limit what employees are doing during work time. But how far can you go in requiring them to act and dress in particular ways when working remotely?

Just like in the office, it's a good idea to give directions around the need to get up from their desk, move and stretch, to avoid injury. This could be an A4 page of sample exercises with a direction to display it at their desk and do the exercises once every hour. Equally, give directions regarding what is not to be done in an ordinary absence/break from work – like hanging out the washing, or perhaps going for a run.

What about clothing? We've all seen people post photos online of their working from home outfits. Suit jacket on top, yoga pants below, and anything from sneakers, to bare feet, to my personal favourite, ugg boots on their feet. But what you require someone to wear is about more than just making sure they look professional on a video Teams meeting. It's about safety too.

> Dale Hargreaves worked for Telstra. She worked from home two days a week (very progressive for 2006!). In August of that year, Dale fell down the stairs and injured her left shoulder. About six

---

38 *Comcare v PVYW* [2013] HCA 41.

weeks later she fell down the stairs again and injured the same shoulder. Both times she said she coughed, lost her balance and fell. Surgery was required, and she later developed depression and anxiety disorders.

Dale made a compensation claim. Telstra denied liability because the injuries occurred away from her workstation and outside typical office hours. The issue was whether her physical injuries arose out of, or in the course of, her employment.

So why was she going down the stairs? Dale explained the first time was to get cough mixture. It was about 6 p.m. and she was still working, logged into the Telstra system remotely, when she began coughing violently. When she went downstairs, she was dressed in casual clothes and wearing socks, but no shoes. She said her decision to get the cough mixture was similar to other breaks, like a toilet break.

The second time she had started work at 8:30 a.m. and then about 8:40 a.m. she went to lock the front door when her son went to school. She wanted to lock the door because Telstra had instructed her to make sure it was locked due to a burglary in the area the year before.

The Tribunal found both falls were in the course of employment and granted the claim.[39]

So where does that leave you? The Tribunal didn't need to consider whether the stairs were dangerous or whether wearing socks contributed to the fall. But you would be wise to consider it.

Safety in the workplace is about more than avoiding workers compensation claims. It's about protecting your employees and complying with workplace safety laws. Nobody wants to know they

---

39 *Hargreaves and Telstra Corporation Limited* [2011] AATA 417 (17 June 2011).

failed to keep someone safe. And nobody wants to be on the end of a prosecution for failure to provide a safe workplace due to not identifying hazards or putting in place ways to remove or minimise them. If stairs are a potential hazard in a workplace, maybe requiring sensible shoes to be worn would be a reasonable way to mitigate any risk.

Another way to avoid these kinds of disputes, is to have clear working hours. This will also help employees stick to boundaries and avoid overwork. I've heard of one company where they enforce this by cutting off access to company systems after office hours. (I think I'd be grateful if someone did this for me!) In France they passed a law in 2017 requiring companies with 50 of more employees to negotiate after hours email rules with employees. For example, not being required to answer emails after hours and on weekends.

While I don't think we are going to see laws like that in Australia any time soon – we are already seeing negative health effects from overwork, and it is likely that companies will start enforcing some clearer boundaries to limit this.

A Homeforce policy is a good place for some general terms around working hours, and more detailed specifications can be set out in an individual contract of employment (which we will discuss in step 4 of the framework).

## 2. WORKING AT HOME PRODUCTIVELY

### Optimise the environment

Once an environment is considered safe, you then need to consider whether it is optimised to help an employee work productively. Talking to one client during the coronavirus pandemic, I found that he came out of the forced work from home periods with a deep-seated aversion to having his small team work from home. Being a tech company I found this rather surprising. Surely they were prime candidates for a fully remote Homeforce? So I dug a little deeper. Turns out he discovered one of the employees was also looking after his one-year-old and three-year-old at home two days each week while he was supposed to be working.

Now, I don't know if you have kids, but I do. They are older now, but I still remember those younger days. If you were lucky, they might have both had a solid two or three-hour nap each day, but other than that those toddlers are active. There is no sitting down at a computer in a noise-free environment. More likely there will be at least one tugging on your legs demanding you come and play, feed them or change their nappy. It is go, go, go.

There is a reason we don't bring our kids into the office with us. It's just not conducive to the environment we need to think clearly and work productively. It's pretty much impossible to be a present parent and a focused, productive worker. Something has to give.[40]

So if you know that an employee has children at home – how are they going to manage that? Is there a partner or other carer there looking after the kids? Is there a separate office with a locked (and soundproof) door? Much as I am strongly against discriminating against team members based on their family responsibilities (not only because it's illegal), it is a pure fact that an employee is employed to work, and needs to be able to do so as effectively as possible. This makes it a fair and reasonable discussion to have with your staff members.

Another example of distractions at home could be having a partner (or housemate) who also works from home. If they are both sharing an office space at home then generally there is nothing

---

40 I appreciate that enforced lockdowns and school closures may force employees into these situations. In that event, I fully encourage employers to give as much compassion and flexibility as possible. However, in 'normal' times when schools and day cares are operational, you don't have to allow working from home when employees are simultaneously caring for their children (or have similar distractions).

different to working in an open-plan office. However, what if they both spend a lot of time on the phone? Are they able to tune each other out, focus, and get on with their own work? Or do they have another room to use for private and quiet conversations?

To open up these conversations with your team, it's best to start with an open-ended question like – on the days you will be working from home, will there be any other people present during your working hours? If they answer *yes*, you might then ask – how will you handle any distraction or disruption? Remember – people work in offices with multiple others all the time. So it is not the mere presence of another person that is the problem. It is who they are and whether they will impact on the employee's ability to work.

What about noise and disruption from outside the office? Is there a new house being built next door? Or a noisy neighbour in the apartment above? Whatever the disruption, the key is for the employee to acknowledge it and have a plan of attack for dealing with it.

## Measuring productivity

Another matter to consider at this point is whether or not you intend to use any technological surveillance tools to monitor employee productivity. This might include GPS tracking devices in company vehicles, fingerprinting, tracking devices on mobile phones (company or personal), video surveillance via webcam, keystroke and internet browser history monitoring.

If you are going to use something like this, or you think you might in future, it's a good idea to consider it now so that you can cover the legal requirements in your Homeforce policy. Given all the states and territories have different requirements I'm going to stick with the high-level principles. In short, you need to make sure you cover three things when planning to use surveillance:

- A legitimate purpose: you can't just use surveillance because you're curious, or because you think it might be handy one day. Legitimate reasons include things such as personal safety (for example, a mobile phone tracking app or device when employees are visiting clients in multiple locations), protecting against theft, and for training purposes.

- Notification: whatever you are using, it is important that you have notified those affected that they are being monitored. For example, signs up to inform of CCTV cameras, including it in written policies and discussion during onboarding and so on.

- Consent: it is always best to have people agree to the monitoring. One way to do this is by asking employees to sign a written policy or include it in their contract of employment.

Once you have the surveillance in place, it is important to make sure that it is used appropriately. Putting something in place to minimise theft, and then using it to discipline an employee, may not meet the legal requirements and could see you facing an unfair dismissal claim where the surveillance data is used and results in termination of employment. So don't be scared to say that the data will be used for multiple purposes – so long as they are legit.

* * *

Whatever your general requirements are for limiting distractions and other techniques to ensure productivity, set them out in a clear manner in the Homeforce policy.

Remember, we are talking about minimum work from home requirements. Just because an employee has children at home for some working days doesn't mean it has to be a flat out *no* to having them work from home. That's when the importance of individual negotiation comes in. For example, changing the hours of work so the employee can work when the kids are asleep.

We will talk more about individual arrangements a bit later.

## 3. USING APPROPRIATE TOOLS AND RESOURCES

In this third section we need to think about the physical and other tools that an employee needs, as a minimum, to be able to work away from a central office. For any knowledge worker the starting point is always: desk, chair, computer of some description, electricity, internet connection, and any necessary software to gain remote access to your work systems. Remember those first panicked coronavirus days when you just sent your employee packing with a laptop? That was absolute bare essentials.

From there you need to think about other essentials that apply specifically to your workforce. For example, if an employee is dealing with hard-copy documents, maybe the employee needs a lockable drawer or cupboard to store them. Maybe they need a printer and scanner to print those documents out, either for signing or just to make them easier to review.

If the employee spends their day reviewing long, complex contract documents maybe it is highly desirable for them to have two big computer screens to more easily see the text. Or maybe they need a tablet to allow for creative work.

Does the employee need a telephone for calls to other staff members, clients or other contacts? Or is talking via wifi sufficient? Maybe a headset with microphone would help if they are on the phone a lot – to enable them to still write or type while they talk. Handsfree doesn't always have the same call quality, and there is nothing more annoying than trying to have a conversation when all you can hear is the fingers on the keyboard.

What about the tools that help make a home office safe? Here you might start thinking about a portable standing desk, a physio fit ball, or a separate keyboard and mouse to avoid an employee being hunched over a laptop screen.

The final level of consideration when it comes to tools and resources are the 'nice to haves'. Whether an employee was in an office or cubicle space, they were probably used to having close access to a whiteboard, pinup board or similar for displaying notes and work tasks. I love having a whiteboard close to my desk so I can quickly glance over at the tasks on my list. What about desk drawers, pens, paper, paperclips and other stationery items? Isn't that part of the fun of working in an office? Being able to raid the stationery cupboard for the latest highlighter colours and other fancy things? How much of these things does an employee need when working from home?

Next step is to think about the software needs. Will the business have one central cloud-based system to keep track of all projects? There are some great project management tools available. Trello and Asana are a couple of generic ones. There are heaps more, and many that are specific to industries like the legal industry.

Aside from telephone and email, what methods of communication are you going to provide? Instant messaging? Chat functions in the project management tool? Some of this you might want to decide on after having reviewed the later steps in this process where we focus on team and manager interactions.

After you've considered all of these questions you should have a nice list of items under the headings 'bare essentials', 'essentials for your business', 'safety requirements' and 'nice to haves', like so:

| Bare essentials | Business essentials | Safety requirements | Nice to haves |
|---|---|---|---|
| Computer<br>Internet<br>Desk<br>Chair | Printer<br>High-speed internet<br>Lockable drawers<br>Phone<br>Basic stationery | Stand up desk<br>Keyboard and mouse | Whiteboard<br>Tablet |

**To pay or not to pay**

At this point you need to make a decision.

What, if any, of these things is your business going to provide to help an employee set up a home office, and what things are you going to require the employee to provide? I suggest you make a little notation next to each item in your table – 'E' for employee provides, 'C' for company provides or 'CC' for company pays a contribution.

The answer here will partly depend on legal requirements, which will be influenced by the reason the employee is working from home. For example, if the employee requests to work remotely, and the employer otherwise provides a fully serviced office, there is no obligation on the business to provide or pay for anything. Also, there's no obligation to pay or provide when a position is offered as a work from home arrangement and it doesn't specify that items will be paid for or provided.

But what if a business has a co-located office and then decides it wants to save money on rent by asking people to work remotely? This doesn't automatically mean employers have to pay for everything. It will depend on various factors, including whether the contract of employment includes the ability to transfer an employee to another location of work (including from home). In many cases there may also be an award obligation to consult with the employees about the changed working arrangements. This consultation may result in negotiated agreements about providing equipment, paying a one-off home set up fee, and perhaps an ongoing allowance. But none of these things are mandated by law.

Things are different again when there is a government mandate to work from home where possible.

In 2020, Mr McKean brought an unfair dismissal claim saying he was forced to resign because his employer directed him to work from home but refused to pay for or provide him with a desk.

It all started in March 2020 when the company sent an email encouraging staff to work from home due to the pandemic. Later staff were told to start making arrangements. Mr McKean said he'd recently moved and had no furniture, including a table or desk to work from. Mr McKean said he was under financial pressure and could not buy a desk. He was allowed to continue to work from the office.

In July 2020, the Victorian Government mandated employees work from home if they could do so. The company provided employees with laptops, chairs, headsets and ergonomic assessments, but did not provide desks. Mr McKean was directed to comply with the work from home direction. He instead requested six weeks leave which was refused due to operational needs. He then resigned.

Mr McKean brought an unfair dismissal claim, which was denied. The Fair Work Commission made it clear that he had other options but to resign. He could've bought the desk he said he could afford. There was no legal obligation on his employer to provide one.[41]

---

41 *McKean v Red Energy Pty Ltd* [2020] FWC 5688.

If you are going to be asking an employee to provide their own devices then it will be worthwhile considering whether to implement a BYO device policy covering the essential issues.

There is no right or wrong answer here. There is currently no law in Australia that prevents you making an agreement to hire someone on the condition they work remotely and provide their own home office. But this may change. So do what feels right now, but keep and eye and ear out for changes to the law. Write up your minimum intentions in your Homeforce policy, and remember – you can always agree something a bit different on an individual basis.

## 4. IMPLEMENTING APPROPRIATE SECURITY MEASURES

As I mentioned before, security matters are often not given the attention they deserve. We all hear about people's personal information being hacked, identities stolen, and companies who get hacked and held to ransom in order to get back access to their data. Or maybe it's your social media account being taken over, or a phishing email. But that's not going to happen to us . . . right? We are just an ordinary person, a small company, surely not worth the trouble?

Unfortunately, these kinds of things do happen to ordinary people. It is also a lot harder to maintain the security and confidentiality of information when it isn't all kept in a central place like a business office.

### Tech security

It's not enough to just believe it won't happen to you. You need to put some essential security measures in place. All of your measures will fit into one of three categories: systems, processes and people, and some will fit into multiple categories.

Now I am definitely not a tech expert. What I have done is list some of the systems and processes that I use in my own business or have learned about in my research. This is not an exhaustive list and I highly recommend you get specialist advice on this. Working in the knowledge industry we are all super reliant on tech. Having it malfunction – or worse be corrupted or held to ransom – would be a nightmare.

Let's look at the issues you will need to address, at a minimum:

- **Systems:** Put in place some key technology security systems such as firewalls, anti-virus protection software, and use of multi-factor authentication. Also, don't forget to acquaint yourself with the security protections you have in the cloud-based software that you are using to make sure you and your staff are following their guidelines.

- **Processes:** The biggest and most obvious security process is password management: what kind of passwords are required, how often they need to be updated, and what to do if you are locked out. A process that goes hand in hand with this is the process for locking your computer when you are away from your desk. Even in crowded offices it is common for people to walk away from their desk leaving their computer unlocked and free for anyone to use. Imagine how much worse people will be in their own home? My kids love hitting a keyboard button here and there, but the last thing I want is for them to accidentally hit send on that email I typed in frustration and was mulling over before a final edit.

  Another big one is internet use. Employees need to know that they must use their own password-protected internet connection. Just because the neighbour next door hasn't wised up to the fact that his wifi connection is unsecured doesn't mean they should use it so they can save their own data for Netflix. Using an unsecured wifi connection makes it very easy for anyone to hack in, and is one of the biggest sources of stolen information. How do you know that your neighbour isn't a hacker luring in

unsuspecting free wifi users so that he can learn all their secrets –
let alone bank details?

- **People:** The biggest worry from a security perspective is
always the people. You can have all the systems and processes in
the world, but if the people don't follow them it doesn't make
a difference. That's why it is super important for your people to
be trained in all of the systems and processes, and for compliance
to be reviewed regularly.

   Make sure they aren't just hitting 'remind me later' for software
   and anti-virus updates, that they are using the secure connections
   and that they know how to identify suspicious emails.

As you can see, running a distributed team means next-level reliance on technology. The last thing you want is it going wrong and
stopping your business. Unless you are a computer whiz yourself,
I recommend that you find and engage a great IT consulting firm
who can be your help desk and make sure that all those updates are
done, and everything stays online and secure.

## Physical security

### Securing premises

It's also easy to forget physical security measures. We've talked about
the potential need to have lockable drawers for company documents,
and a lockable door on the home office. The need for a private area
for the workstation and to ensure that no one else in the premises is
viewing the on-screen data.

But what about the whole house or apartment? Is the property
adequately secured? Is a locked front door enough, or do you want
alarms? Maybe video cameras outside? You really can go all out here.
Although I'd strongly suggest that if you aren't worried about alarms
and video cameras in the workplace office then you can hardly
argue that an employee needs them at home. And again, who pays?

## Mobile phones

Let's think about mobile phones too. It's the rare person these days who doesn't have their work email on their phone. If they don't, it's usually because it's either not permitted by the company, or more often, the employee has made a deliberate decision to remove the mailbox from their phone to stop themselves from checking it all the time. Remember that concept of 'boundaries'? Mobile phones are a major contributor to poor boundaries.

So assuming your company is one of the majority that allows company email on personal mobile phones, and the employee hasn't removed it, how do you handle the security? What if the phone is lost or stolen? How is the data protected? The options include everything from requiring phones to be password-protected before mailboxes are loaded, signing agreements to require employees to inform the company immediately if there is a lost or stolen phone so the data link can be disabled, or even just providing the employee with a work mobile phone so you have complete control over it.

This last idea of providing the phone is also good if you are trying to protect other company information, like client contact details. As a business owner my phone is full of contacts that are work related. If you are asking your employees to use their phone for work purposes it is pretty common to find they save a number so they know who a repeat caller is. When the employee leaves the business, those numbers don't magically disappear out of their phone. So how do you stop them walking away with those contact details and perhaps trying to claim that client as their own? Also, your clients will now have the mobile phone number of that employee. So how can you stop them from calling that employee directly? You can't.

If these questions throw up concerns for you then it is definitely worth considering providing a mobile phone to your employees. When they leave you simply have them return the phone and you pass it along to the next employee who fills the role. You can never know if someone has gone to the trouble of downloading the data, but you can sure make it harder for them to keep the data by not allowing them to keep the phone.

## Employee consent

It's going to be difficult to do a lot of what's required to maintain security without the consent of your employee. For example, your employee is going to need to engage with that IT consulting firm you hire so you will need their agreement to allow the IT consulting firm access to their equipment when required. Don't forget to cover this in your Homeforce policy.

## 5. CHOOSING APPROPRIATE INSURANCE

Last, but certainly not least, you need to consider insurance. The insurance will need to cover any concerns you have about the health of the employee, physical damage to your property or the employee's property while the employee is working remotely, and potentially, injury to third parties.

## Workers' compensation

In every State and Territory in Australia, regardless of where an employee is working, you have the obligation to have some form of workers compensation insurance. In simple terms, this insurance will kick in when an employee becomes ill or injured and their work or workplace has been a contributing factor to that illness or injury. So if an employee becomes mentally unwell as a result of bullying in the workplace, they can bring a workers compensation claim. If the employee trips over the cables from their computer, and twists an ankle, they can bring a workers compensation claim. This is regardless of whether the employee knew better than to leave cables laying around as a trip hazard. It's a no-fault jurisdiction. So even if you as the employer are not to blame, the employee can still bring a claim.

## Property damage

What about damage to property? Most employees will have some form of home and contents insurance. But not everyone. Some people choose not to worry about insurance because they believe the chance of damage is slim and they would rather pocket the money and use it in other ways. So where does that leave you if someone breaks into your employee's house and steals the computer or printer you provided? Or damages the chair and desk? Not in a good place. It will likely be significantly harder to get the money for the computer from your employee when compared to an insurance company.

## Public liability

Speaking of personal insurance – does the employee's home insurance (if they have it) extend to liability if someone is injured on their property? For example, what if the employee receives a delivery from a courier with work documents, and the courier trips over the unsafe front step and breaks their ankle?

## Decide your risk appetite

Do you want to take the risk that an employee has the proper insurances in place, or would you prefer to take responsibility and control and just do what needs doing to feel secure that you are completely covered?

Everyone's answer to that will be different. This is really where you need to know yourself and what level of risk you are prepared to accept. Start with talking to a good insurance broker about the risks that you are insured for when your team is distributed. Ask that same broker what insurance an employee can get. Look at the costs for each.

Analyse each of the risks and determine which ones you think are most likely to happen, how serious the consequences will be if things go wrong, and also what it would take (time, money, equipment) for you to minimise that risk. Sound familiar? Yep — it's just a straight-up risk analysis.

What are you prepared to insure for and what do you expect the distributed employee to insure for? Make sure you clearly specify this in your Homeforce policy.

## PUTTING IT ALL TOGETHER IN A HOMEFORCE POLICY

All of the thinking you've just been doing around these five essential areas has been for the purpose of helping you design the essential foundations for your distributed team.

Now for the easy part.

With all of those thoughts and the notes you've made you are now ready to start writing your Homeforce policy. These are the key requirements that apply to all employees (subject to any individual negotiations). Your goal is to have all employees complying with this policy. To help you with this, and as a thank you for purchasing this book, I've created a framework for a Homeforce policy covering each of these topics and leaving room for you to vary it to suit your needs. You can access a copy of that free template at 3dhrlegal.com. au/homeforce/resources.

## Step 3 summary

- Spend some quiet time considering each of the five essential issues of remote work:
    - Working at home safely
    - Working at home productively
    - Using appropriate tools and resources
    - Implementing appropriate safety measures
    - Choosing appropriate insurance
- Take your notes and create your remote work (Homeforce) policy.

# CHAPTER 7

# Step 4: Organise your team

'The competitions to hire the best will increase in the years ahead.
Companies that give extra flexibility to their employees will have
the edge in this area.'

Bill Gates

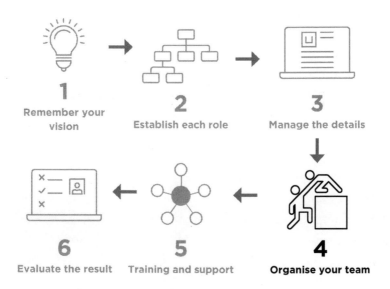

**1**
Remember your
vision

**2**
Establish each role

**3**
Manage the details

**6**
Evaluate the result

**5**
Training and support

**4**
Organise your team

## SELECTING THE RIGHT PERSON

People aren't robots. The previous step in the REMOTE Framework had you considering the five key issues when it comes to a distributed team, and working out your ideal scenario. For example – you'd love all of your team members to have a separate workstation with a lockable door to the room. But life isn't perfect. You can't always get what you want (just ask Mick Jagger). We are dealing with humans and their varied personalities and ways of living.

Step 4 is all about considering the individual person, selecting only those best suited to work in a distributed fashion, and negotiating the terms where appropriate.

Now that you have determined a particular role can be worked remotely, and created your preferred Homeforce conditions policy, you know the minimum requirements an employee needs to meet. However, before you start asking them about their office set up, there is one more step: you need to *select the right people*.

Remember at the beginning of this book we discussed examples of people who are not suited to work from home? There were physical reasons, like a lack of private space. There were also mental reasons why a person is not suited to work from home, like the employee who just can't focus on their own or motivate themselves without the support of a team.

So, for every individual in your business, or who you are thinking about hiring, you need to go through a selection process. Before you can select anyone, there are two key questions to answer:

- Does this person have the physical environment suited to work from home?

- Do they have the key characteristics of conscientiousness, emotional regulation and influence, looked at in chapter 2, to show they are mentally suited?

Now you might be a good judge of character, but I'd say having a guess here is not the best way to go. So, what can you do?

## THE APPLICATION PROCESS

If you are recruiting for a new role you will likely advertise and ask all interested people to submit an application. I'd start by getting something in writing, or a video if you're up for asking for it. Don't stop at asking for a CV and a cover letter. Ask everyone to address their suitability to work in a distributed team (whether hybrid or not), and make clear it's a key requirement. Ask them how they will be a productive, engaged and connected team member if working in a distributed team. It's a waste of time for everyone involved if the person only wants to work in a central office.

Now this is an obvious first step for a new employee – but don't discount it for an existing employee. The Homeforce process isn't about someone casually working from home a random day here or there, or doing a bit of work on a working holiday. It's about embedding a continuous distributed work team. You want to make sure your current people are as equally committed as any new person who joins the team. Ask them to fill in a modified job application that just focuses on how they will handle doing their job remotely. Once you've received and read your applications – decide who proceeds to the next selection stage.

### Go back to basics – do an interview

Next step is an interview process.

For a new employee, asking about their ability to work in a distributed team needs to be a formal part of the structured interview plan, not just a throwaway line about the option or requirement to work remotely.

For existing employees it needs to be more than just a casual chat in the office. Being flexible and a good employer in today's market doesn't mean just saying 'yes' whenever you get a request to work outside the office. That's not doing anyone any favours. Changing to a distributed arrangement is a big adjustment for any person.

During the interview, ask questions like:

- 'Do you like working from home?'
- 'What do you find the challenges to be?'
- 'How do you motivate yourself and avoid distractions?'
- 'How do you like communicating with your team?'
- 'Do you have any rules in place with your family when you are working at home?'
- 'What office environment do you have set up?'
- 'What is your technology situation? Computer, internet and so on.'

Give them some specific scenarios and see how they handle them.

### Personality testing

Another selection option to determine individual 'fit' is a personality test.

While some people do not take them seriously, I truly believe that there is benefit in using a personality test. It does give you some insights. But I don't recommend using it as a method to rule someone out from being offered the opportunity to join your distributed team. There is no perfect score or perfect answer. A personality test is a source of information you can use to start a conversation.

Use it as a guide to work out where a person might have some struggles. For example, if the test shows they like to be the centre of the social circle – how can you make sure that this person still gets enough social contact and interactions with others at work to prevent feelings of loneliness and isolation kicking in? Or perhaps you need to help them ensure that they get that interaction outside work.

Or maybe you will find the person struggles with focus. In that case, perhaps it is a matter of suggesting technology or other strategies. For example, apps on your computer and devices – like Offtime, Freedom and AppBlock – that stop you from logging into social media accounts for set periods of time. Or perhaps some more physical boundaries like time blocking to help the employee stay on task rather than wandering off to do the laundry.

A personality test is an opportunity to learn about someone, have a discussion and work out if there is a way to remove or remedy any possible challenges for that individual. It's always better to be forewarned and have a plan.

### What kind of test to use?

As mentioned earlier, there are so many different personality tests. There are the classics like the Myers–Briggs Test, the DiSC test and 16 Personalities. Then there are all sorts of tests that various different business coaches, trainers and recruiters like to use. Here's a few of the more popular ones that I've tried or had recommended, and which you might like to explore:

- the Clifton Strengths test (my personal favourite)
- The Hogan Assessments
- Click colours
- the Enneagram test
- the Kolbe index.

I'm not recommending any particular test here. The most important thing is to choose one that suits your purpose of figuring out if someone will work well in a distributed team. Do some research. Be clear what characteristics and traits you are testing for. Read about each test. How long has it been in existence? Is there any scientific research to support its use? Is there scientific research that debunks the test? How are people categorised under the test? What level of personality detail does it show? Does it test for the characteristics you want?

After you've picked a few that you like, test them on yourself. How easy was the test to take? Did it take a long time? What cost was involved? What about the results – were they reflective of your personality? Are you a blue, red, green or yellow? What is your highest strength? Where are your weaknesses? Are you an introvert or extrovert?

The answers might surprise you. Show the results to someone close to you and ask them whether they think the results are reflective of who you are. It is a common human weakness that we don't always have true insight into ourselves, or at least don't see ourselves the way others do.

After all this reading, testing and talking, you should be in a good position to choose a test. Weigh up the costs, time involved, relevancy to your outcome, and pick the one best suited to test for a person who will work well in your distributed team.

## Putting it all together

If you are keen to use a personality test, I recommend it be the second step – not the first. Personality tests are often used in recruiting to help a decision maker whittle down the number of people who are suitable for interview. However, I think doing a personality test too early can give you preconceived ideas – and remember, they are just a point-in-time test.

If you really like someone in an interview and the personality test shows up some concerns then use the test results as an opportunity to have a further conversation with the individual. Share the results with the person and give them some time to consider them, and then hold a follow-up meeting (a more unstructured interview) to discuss any points of concern. The purpose of the meeting is not to say, 'This test shows you can't function in a distributed team.' Instead, you are pointing out the concerns and working together to see if you can create some strategies to minimise those concerns.

Even if there are no obvious concerns, the test results give you something else to discuss in a second interview, which I always recommend. It might even make the candidate a little more talkative – everyone loves learning about themselves, right?

## Other selection options

Applications, interviews and personality tests aren't the only selection methods available to determine suitability for a distributed role. It might be enough for you, but if you want to add anything else (such as group activities, group interviews or work tests) then don't be shy. The only 'must do' for new hires is a reference check. At the very least I recommend an application (CV, cover letter, selection criteria), a personality test, an interview and a reference check.

There is a reason people say, 'hire slow, fire fast'. You invest a lot of time and money in your team and new hires can have a big positive (or negative) influence on it in a short time. So take your time and make sure you are comfortable before you commit. Turnover costs big.

## Trial it

Your commitment to a remote working arrangement doesn't have to be for the long term. Whether we are talking about new employees or existing ones moving to a distributed style of work, it's a good idea to 'trial it'. You might call it a probation period, trial or test. It doesn't really matter. What matters is that it's an opportunity for both of you to see what works, what doesn't and what can be improved.

The great thing about a trial period is that you start with the expectation that things aren't going to be perfect. Setting your expectations lower makes the whole experience more relaxed. It doesn't mean employees can slack off. It just means when teething problems arise people are not so ready to blame – they are more likely to approach those issues from a problem-solving perspective.

## CONTRACTS OF EMPLOYMENT

Now that you've selected your person, it's time to record your agreement and your expectations in writing. You've already made a headstart having done a position description and a distributed work policy, so now it's time to go to the individual level. Yes – I'm talking about a contract of employment.

If you are sitting there thinking to yourself, *but we don't have written contracts of employment* – stop right there. A written contract of employment is the one essential document I believe *all* employers need to have with their employees. Whether it is a two-page highlights style, a 20-page document including everything and the kitchen sink, or something in between, you really need to have something. Preferably a document that accurately and clearly records all the terms you've agreed with the employee.

Whether you have something in writing or not, when you have an employment relationship there is a contract between you. It is the foundation of your relationship. Why would you choose to rely on a verbal agreement and a handshake when we all know that two people can have a conversation and come away from it believing two different things were agreed? A written contract of employment provides clarity for you and the employee.

I know some people don't like to have written contracts – or anything at all in writing – because they believe it removes flexibility. Not so. Remember our discussion about position descriptions?

Just because it's in writing doesn't mean you can't change it. For example, in your contract of employment you might like to make it a requirement that a working from home arrangement is not a contractual right – rather it is a privilege that you can decide to remove in certain circumstances, such as poor performance.

This is also something you will want to remember when it comes to flexible work requests under the NES. Such requests are only valid when a person falls within one of the grounds for making a request (such as children school aged or younger). So what happens if that changes? Can the employee who wanted to work part time for the last 10 years while they were caring for their elderly parents suddenly demand they return to full-time work? Can the employer demand it of them? The answer depends on whether their contract of employment was changed to part time in a substantive capacity, or whether it was always expressed as being a temporary arrangement subject to change by either party.

Also – there are some things that unless they are in writing just don't exist. For example, a restraint of trade. There is no law that says an employee can't chase your clients, or try to steal your employees, or set up in competition with you after their employment ends. If you want to stop that kind of conduct you need to have the employee agree in writing.

### Designing a contract to suit an individual

Now that you're on board with having a written contract of employment, it's time to get back to considering how it needs to look to accommodate a distributed, flexible work arrangement. This is also where you have the opportunity to negotiate terms that vary your Homeforce policy.

For example, perhaps you have a general requirement in your policy that all employees provide their own computer. This might be fine in the majority of cases, but perhaps one employee asks you to provide them with a computer because their personal computer is used by the whole family and they can't afford to purchase a new one. There are a range of options here. You might be able to loan the employee the money for the purchase and slowly deduct it from their salary. You might allow the employee to salary sacrifice to purchase a new computer, which will reduce the cost to them. Or perhaps you might just outright provide it.

Another example is the mobile phone. Perhaps you have made a blanket decision that you will provide all employees with a company phone. A new employee may approach you wanting to use their own phone and number because they are coming from another business and bringing their old clients with them who already know that number. In that case, you might start talking about providing the employee with a phone allowance instead.

What about something less tangible? The employee who has three kids who are all at school and they don't leave until 8:30 a.m. and are home by 3:30 p.m. every day? That only leaves about 6.5 hours of working time, and they find they get dragged into the melee in the rush to get ready in the morning, and the need from the kids when they get home to immediately share everything about their day. Perhaps this employee wants to start work at 5 a.m. and work till 7 a.m. before the kids are awake, and then complete the rest of their work hours during the school hours, meaning they finish before the usual office closing time each day.

You might have guessed – I'm actually talking about myself here. This is exactly my situation. I might not always be great at finishing at 3:30 p.m. I might take a break and find myself back at the computer within a half hour, or perhaps I will just be taking sneaky glances at my phone, but roughly this is the schedule I try to work to. Especially while I'm trying to write this book.

Is this kind of arrangement something that you would willingly agree to with an employee? Whatever the individual circumstances are — and whatever you agree to — where it is something different to the baseline you have established it's important to record it in writing. This kind of personal arrangement needs to go in a contract of employment, or at least a letter of variation to the base contract of employment that already exists.

You don't want to be arguing down the track. Maybe it will be an employee who says you told them they could perform their 38 hours of work whenever they wanted to, when you in fact need them available during standard office hours. It's hardly going to work for you if they decide to work when it suits them and it's 5 a.m. till 9 a.m. and 7 p.m. till 11 p.m.

Put the guidelines into place, clearly and accurately in writing. Don't let yourself be caught in an argument that is all 'he said', 'she said'. We all know how that ends. Get yourself a good lawyer and have an employment contract drafted that meets legal requirements and suits all of the personal goals of the business. Don't leave it to chance that the template you found on the internet will pass muster if it gets tested.

Don't forget! This whole distributed work arrangement for a particular individual can be on a trial basis. If that's what you want — you must put it in writing with clear steps as to how the deal can be terminated, and what happens next.

---

## Step 4 summary

- Determine if an individual employee is suited to work from home. Use applications, interviews and personality tests.

- Agree on any individual conditions, and make sure all staff have clear and current contracts of employment.

---

# CHAPTER 8

# Step 5: Training and support

'Growth and comfort do not coexist.'
Ginni Rometty

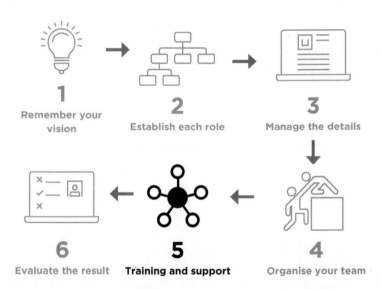

**1** Remember your vision

**2** Establish each role

**3** Manage the details

**6** Evaluate the result

**5** Training and support

**4** Organise your team

At this point in the process towards building a Homeforce you're likely already feeling like you've achieved a lot. You've gotten artistic and designed your vision, you've assessed your whole workforce structure and all individual jobs, you've assessed and spoken to all of your existing employees, and you've put in place the three key documents that form the basis of the distributed team relationship with each staff member: a Homeforce policy, a job description and a contract of employment.

Phew.

In short, you are now set up for success.

The next step is to focus on all of the individuals in your business. We're going to look at them in two categories – employees and managers.

## EMPLOYEE TRAINING AND SUPPORT

I often say to my clients that an employment relationship is like a marriage. We all go into marriage in love, dreaming of a long future and growing old together. We might notice some flaws, but we are unconcerned, believing love conquers all. Then reality sets in. Picking up the dirty towel on the bathroom floor becomes a chore not an expression of love, the quirks – like butting in when you are talking – stop being seen as someone with lots of information to share and start seeming rude.

In an employment relationship we might be starry-eyed about a person's job history or rare skills and see only the benefits the employee can bring to our business. What at first is seen as a strong leadership style might later be viewed as aggressive and bullying.

In both cases we don't spend enough time thinking about what might go wrong, how to keep the relationship healthy, and importantly, planning the exit if it becomes necessary.

Relationships take ongoing work. It is not a set-and-forget kind of thing. Just ask all those marriage counsellors out there. Unfortunately, there isn't really a similar thing for employment relationships. You're not likely to ask your employee to go to counselling with you.

Employment relationships typically get managed in house. If things go wrong, the likely result is that someone will end the relationship and move on. Sometimes that is absolutely the best outcome. However, we are trying to avoid turnover here, so we need some strategies to start the relationship off on the right foot, and keep it on track for years, not just months.

Also – let's not forget that a marriage has one big advantage. There are only two people involved (well, usually). Whereas in the workplace – there might be hundreds of people and dozens of different interconnecting relationships.

The starting point is to make sure that all of the individual employees start off on the right foot and have the skills and tools to develop successful relationships with their managers, their team and themselves. Focusing on employees during this step in the Homeforce process, there are three key areas of focus:

- onboarding
- managing ongoing interactions
- individual remote work skills.

### Employee training and support step 1: onboarding

Many people think of an onboarding program starting from an employee's first day of work. In my view it starts much earlier than that. In truth, it starts from the very first contact that your employee has with your business.

The interview? No.

The job advertisement? Maybe not.

It's actually any contact that your employee has had with your business and brand before they start to work for you.

I recently went through the recruitment process to take on a new lawyer in my team. It surprised and delighted me that one of the candidates specifically said that she'd been aware of my business and me through my work co-hosting 'The Juggle' podcast, had followed me as a result, and had ultimately decided to apply for the job because of those prior interactions.

Two other candidates stated that the job advertisement 'spoke to them'. They weren't looking for 'big law'. They liked our innovative service model and product offerings and felt that the firm I described in my ad was something they would be keen to have created themselves and were excited to be a part of.

The point I want to get across here is that how you present to your employees early on in a relationship sets the tone for the rest of it. So when you are hiring, make sure the job advertisement truly reflects the kind of business you run – the company values, how you like to work with clients, the team culture that underpins the business. Make sure that your interview questions don't just focus on technical skills but also go towards cultural fit.

Then when you are ready to make an offer, don't spoil it by sending a letter and contract of employment that is at odds with your image. If you are direct and plain speaking, don't send a contract that is 20 pages long and uses old-fashioned words like 'recitals' and 'hereto'. Every touchpoint with your new employee should be considered. We've all heard of customer experience – but don't forget about employee experience. A poor employee experience is just as much a killer of your business as a poor customer experience. And your onboarding process is a key component that can set the new relationship up for success or failure.

### Onboarding remote workers

Onboarding programs are not created equal. In some businesses an onboarding program looks like the employee being greeted at reception on the first day, given a tour of the office premises and introduced to all the staff (or at least the staff in their team), before being shown to their desk and given some work.

Other onboarding programs last a whole week. They start with a tour, include scheduled training in various software systems, time with finance to make sure all the employment paperwork has been completed correctly, time spent with human resources or management reviewing all of the company policies and procedures, and maybe include a morning coffee or lunch with the employee's new manager or whole team.

The extent of your onboarding system is totally up to you. Consider the size of your business, your number of employees, the complexity of your systems and determine the best onboarding process for you. Is it all going to be handled remotely? Do you prefer for your onboarding to all be done in person? Is that even possible in some cases? Do you want to have a preferred onboarding system that allows for variation in certain circumstances?

Although it's important to have someone who takes responsibility for the entire onboarding process, don't just delegate the entire creation of the process to someone else. Give some real time to consider what the best onboarding system looks like for onboarding a Homeforce in your business.

Every time a new employee starts in your Homeforce (whether they are an existing employee or not) they need to be trained – not just in how to do their job, but how everything works in your organisation. An employee who has been working with you already in an office environment will clearly have a head start as they are familiar with the business and the job they are required to do. But that doesn't mean they don't still need to be onboarded. Changing to a remote working arrangement isn't as simple as handing them a laptop and telling them to keep doing what they are doing – just do it from home.

\* \* \*

There are three key considerations to a great onboarding process. The technical requirements, the in-person meetings and initial training, and the overall employee experience. Plan to cover each requirement in your onboarding process, especially whether it is going to be handled remotely or in person.

## The technical requirements

First – the technical requirements. What are the essential things that you need to tick off with an employee when they start working with you? At a minimum, this would include the general paperwork review – checking tax file declarations and contracts have been signed and returned, and allowing the employee some time to read and ask questions on company policies like codes of conduct and complaint management procedures. Depending on the size of your business this might be handled by your office manager, HR team or you.

Don't skip over the time that an employee gets to spend reading through company policies and procedures – especially a code of conduct if you have one (which I highly recommend). These documents are directions about how you want people to work within your business, and how you want them to relate to other employees and clients.

It is so incredibly important to set these standards and expectations and to enforce them upfront. It is easier to start someone on the right path than it is to get them to change direction later on. I once spent over a year working with a local government on various issues which all came from staff working in one area together, and all related to bullying disputes because people had made up their own minds about what other people's jobs were, they complained and gossiped amongst themselves, and managers didn't have the skills to address the behaviour.

After various investigations, threats of legal action, and a whole heap of tears, the executive felt there was no option but to start again. Ultimately the actions taken led to a number of voluntary resignations and also some of the employees being fired.

So spend the time up front. Make sure employees know what's expected. Then it's the manager's job to make sure they continue to comply. Get your onboarding process streamlined with a standard process.[42]

### In-person meetings and initial training

Once the paperwork is out of the way and the groundwork is set, the second thing is the in-person contact. Who does the employee need to meet with on their first day, in their first week and in their first month?

On the first day, at a minimum there needs to be a meeting between the employee and their manager – whom they should already have met at some point during the recruitment process – followed by a welcome meeting with their whole team. Where team members are working part time it is important to ensure that the new starter gets an opportunity to meet everyone on their first available working day.

I also strongly recommend that you implement a buddy system. This isn't an unusual step, but it is one that can have a great impact when a person is going to work in a distributed team and doesn't have the ability to just watch and take in the office dynamics. Allocate each new starter a 'buddy' or 'guide' who is not their manager. This person is ideally a peer who has been with the company long enough to know and understand how the company and the people in it like to operate. They might be in the same team, or do a similar job in another team. It could be anyone you like – so long as you know that they have a caring nature and will be a good source of information and direction to the new employee. Someone who you

---

42 You can get a head start with our First Time Employer Pack. Then add your specific company requirements and you will be set.

can train to check in with the new starter and encourage the endless questions that new employees usually have.

In the meetings with the manager and the buddy, it's also a great idea to make sure the manager and buddy have been directed to speak openly about company expectations that might not be said or written elsewhere like in a company code of conduct. For example, etiquette (such as dress code and who speaks when) on virtual conferences and how to use the communication channels. Often more importantly, encourage them to talk about issues such as office politics – who has worked there for a long time? Who are friends with who? What would be an obvious faux pas?

If you are not this person's manager and so haven't spent time with them yet, depending on the size of your business you might also make some time to meet with the new starter yourself. Worried about what you would say? Don't be. You are there to show the employee that you are deeply involved and committed to the business, to represent in person the values that you hold and want others to commit to, and to make the new employee feel welcome. This is leadership by example. You want all of your managers to take note of the importance of training and relationship management, and the need to invest time in it.

These meetings are about making it clear to the new starter that they are important as individuals – not just because of the work they will produce.

### Overall employee experience

The third thing is considering the whole employee experience. When a person starts a job in an office they usually get a tour and see a lot of faces, and then are eventually led to their workstation where someone will hopefully have left them with pens, paper, a computer set up ready to operate, and a working telephone. Some organisations go that little bit further and might leave some flowers or something else on the desk.

When onboarding someone remotely, the key is to think about how you can create opportunities for an employee to experience this same level of connection and welcome. Starting a new job is a prime opportunity to create moments that matter that will stay with an employee for a long time. Rather than having a note on their desk, why not send them a package by courier due to arrive 30 minutes before their official start time on the first day of work? You might include the stationery items the employee will need, a biscuit for morning tea, tea bags or coffee, branded company merchandise, and importantly, a handwritten note from you welcoming them to the business.

Given that the majority of meetings will likely occur via video conferencing, what can you provide to the employee to make those meetings more interesting? Perhaps some cards with emojis or other signals that people can hold up during the meeting? Thumbs up, smiley face, question mark, and anything else you can think of. Throw all of these in the welcome box too and bring a smile to your new employee's face on their first day. Or perhaps spread these gifts out over the course of a week or month to keep the delight going.

The same goes for any existing employees who are being transferred to a working from home arrangement. Don't just hand them the box as they walk out the door on their last day in the office – courier it to their home. Yes, it costs a little more, but that little bit of extra care and attention is what creates a great experience for an employee. It builds connection and ultimately makes them more loyal to your business.

An added bonus of all of this is that employees talk. If they have a great experience working for your business, they are more likely to share about it which will indirectly encourage those in their circle to do business with you, or perhaps to want to work with you too.

**Employee training and support step 2: ongoing interactions**

Just like a honeymoon, those initial days can be super sweet with all of the scheduled gifts, meetings and one-to-one attention, and lead to a big thud down into reality when they are over. The initial onboarding program creates a bond, however if nothing is put in place to manage and reinforce the relationship, it can still come unstuck.

A huge part of a successful ongoing relationship is the manager. Gallup research shows that when it comes to a distributed team, the biggest impact on individual success comes down to one role: the manager (which may be you). That's why the second part of this step in the Framework is dedicated to how to create great managers.

But it's not *all* down to the relevant manager. They still need to take their cue from the company leadership. From you. A business is made up of a lot more than a bunch of individuals. More than a bunch of individual teams. It is an interconnected web that needs to have strong connections across teams for best productivity.

In larger companies, after the employee has started to settle in, it's a good idea to schedule in some meetings between the employee and members of other teams – even teams that the employee won't necessarily be working with directly. There won't be any accidental bumping into a 'new person' in the kitchen or hallway, and introductions being exchanged, so it is necessary to schedule these accidental meetings. This will help the employee feel part of the wider company, will benefit any collaboration that may be required and help the employee perform at a higher level.

You can also encourage communication and connection across teams by putting in place some whole-team social interaction. Some of the examples I've come across include a zoom lunchroom which is always open during the usual lunch hour for people to come and go as they please. The great thing about this is that it resembles the random interaction you get walking into a lunchroom in an office – you never know who you will see and get a chance to talk to.

Another idea is more structured whole-business social events. For example, quiz shows at lunchtime where employees are randomly grouped with other employees. Pet parades. Friday night drinks or dance parties. Dance like no one's watching in your living room? Or holding get-togethers to mark special milestones like birthdays, engagements or work anniversaries. Or maybe it is smaller, more intimate cross-team get-togethers, like speed dating via Zoom.

Whatever you choose, the aim of the game is to ensure that all individuals feel valued and a part of the greater business, not just in a small silo unconnected from the rest.

It's not all just about social interactions either.

Emma Walsh, CEO of Parents At Work, said in an interview that they have implemented 'downtime days' for staff. Where they identify that a staff member has been experiencing a particularly demanding time (whether at work or home), they allocate them a 'downtime day'.

She said, 'That means that we don't ring them. We don't email them. We don't expect them to email or call us ... And we're certainly not going to interrupt them and we're not going to invite them to be at any meetings or in fact, load up their inbox with a whole lot of emails.'

Seemingly small initiatives like this can make a vast impact on how valued an employee feels, promotes loyalty and will likely increase productivity as staff get a chance to recuperate with a bit of quiet time. As Emma said, 'We all need that.'

### Employee training and support step 3: developing individual remote work skills

Finally, in order to truly set an individual up for success in a distributed team, they need to have the knowledge and skills to create a positive working experience for themselves and others in their team.

Employees in a distributed team are likely to be spending more time alone than perhaps they ever have. Not only are they alone, but they are often bringing their work, their office, into their home. People might have worked from home before on an ad hoc basis, maybe bringing the work laptop home overnight or for a weekend and doing a bit of work. But it comes home and goes back again. There is still a clear line that work is at work, and home is home.

This is totally not the case with a Homeforce. The boundaries can be unclear or nonexistent. I know from my own experience that it is really easy for me to just slip into work mode at any time. I have my work emails on my phone, I have a small workstation in a work zone set up for me and the kids which is just off the main living area without a lockable door, and I use the one mobile number for work and personal use. This is a very common set up for many business owners and people who work from home.

I recently saw a *New Yorker* cartoon by David Sipress with a caption which perfectly described this situation: 'I can't remember – do I work at home or do I live at work?' This is not the experience we want for our employees.

We've already discussed some of the risks to employees. Loneliness, disconnection and disengagement. There can also be a risk that employees will work too much. *Yahoo!* you might be thinking. A plus for productivity. For a short while this might be great. However, in the long run it can lead to employee overwhelm and burnout, which is very bad for them and for you.

Although your employees are adults (I assume in most cases) and responsible for their own choices, it is still your business to lead and you are responsible as the owner and/or manager for setting the expectations that drive the work culture. If you're sending and answering emails at 11 p.m., maybe you're sending a message that you expect that from your team. You need to be careful what messages you are sending – and make sure they are consistent. Telling people not to work past 6 p.m. and then doing the opposite yourself is one example.

So, work out what your culture is, set your expectations and communicate consistently. Part of this will involve helping your employees with setting their own boundaries.

In terms of physical set up, while you can recommend some things, other than for safety reasons you can't do much to influence them. If they want to have their desk in their lounge room that's pretty much their choice. You might share images of home work environments that you think are good examples, maybe featuring plants, a standing desk, colourful wall art and that lockable door. Explain why these are good choices – the positive impact of plants and colour on mental health, for example. However, it really is their choice.

## Work from home tips

You can also give them some training around working from home. A quick Google search of 'tips for working from home' will have you turning up thousands of articles, podcasts and books with hundreds of tips. If you're feeling overwhelmed you might start with some of the resources I've listed at the back of this book.

Some of my favourite tips are:

- Make sure you get 'dressed' for work before starting the workday. No more pyjamas at work.

- Choose a clear time for when work starts and stops each day.

- Stick to a routine with planned breaks that don't just revolve around moving to another screen (go for a walk, or do the washing up if you consider that a break).

- If you can, have a separate room for your 'office' and make sure that you close the door (and lock it for good measure) when work is finished for the day. If it isn't a separate room, do what you can to 'pack away' your work desk. Perhaps have a box for all your work things which you unpack and pack each day.

- Limit distractions. This might mean closing the door of the laundry or junk room that you walk past on the way to the bathroom. Or perhaps wearing headphones to block out noisy neighbours.

- Have a ritual that you complete at the end of the day to make sure your mind has time to go from work mode to home mode. This transition time becomes your virtual commute during which you can switch off from work mentally. It might be cooking dinner, crafting or something else that uses different skills.

- Ensure that your work desk doesn't also have personal life admin all over it. Keep work separate.

- Plan some in-person contact with friends and family, or even colleagues, each week to ensure you are getting enough face-to-face contact.

- Doing something to make yourself laugh as it makes you feel good and we do a lot less of it alone. It might be watching funny videos (cat filter video anyone?), your favourite episode of *Seinfeld*, or calling the person who always makes you laugh.

- Plan in some movement. Whether you set a timer to do some stretches every hour, you plan a midday walk, or perhaps you just love a fast and furious dance around the living room for 15 minutes each day. Whatever works for you.

Employees may also need to learn to get comfortable collaborating in a whole new way – whether they are working remotely themselves, or working in a team with people who are distributed elsewhere. Perhaps you can consider implementing training to boost collaboration skills across locations.[43] The last thing you want is for your company to become the next viral video. While it's funny watching lawyers stuck in a cat filter, that's not the kind of publicity we want for our firm.[44] Give your people the skills they need to avoid those embarrassing moments and make themselves as effective as possible.

You can provide training in a range of different ways. You might like to include an initial live training session as part of the induction program, you might prefer to wait until they've settled in a bit, or perhaps you just want to have a recorded training session that is a compulsory watch during the first three months of employment.

This kind of training will go a long way to helping your employees be successful in a distributed team, and equally important, show that you are dedicated to ensuring their success in a healthy way. As an added bonus, there is a correlation between higher productivity and those employees who are given clear work expectations, workers who create daily goals and have structure to their day, and those who receive encouragement to create a routine and specific workspace.[45]

However, don't forget that the responsibility isn't on the employee alone. It's one thing to give some tips and training, but it's also great to provide your employees with the tools they require to get help

---

43 'The Expectation Gap in the Future of Work', Boston Consulting Group, 14 December 2020, (www.bcg.com/en-au/publications/2020/understanding-the-expectation-gap-in-the-future-of-work-australia).

44 If you haven't seen the cat filter video, I highly recommend watching it for a good laugh: https://www.youtube.com/watch?v=lGOofzZOyl8.

45 'Key Working from Home Trends Emerging from COVID-19 – A Report to the Fair Work Commission', Dr John Hopkins and Professor Anne Bardoel, Swinburne University of Technology, November 2020 (www.fwc.gov.au/documents/sites/clerks-work-from-home/research/am202098-research-reference-list-su-241120.pdf).

when needed. Things like making sure their managers are trained to look for signs of employees having difficulty working from home, and training to know when and how to ask questions. Perhaps you can even go so far as to provide access to counselling services from employee assistance providers. The understanding of the importance of managing potential mental health concerns has been growing over the last twenty years, and it is only becoming more important as we move to new ways of working.

There is an obvious equation – if your employees aren't well they won't be functioning at top capacity and their productivity, and therefore your business revenue, will be affected. However, given you're reading this book, I am pretty sure that you know it is more than this. I feel that it's our duty as leaders to create not only a safe place to work, but also one where they feel cared for as a human being with a whole life that exists outside what they do for us each day. It's important to make sure that their work doesn't negatively impact that, and in fact, enhances it.

## MANAGER TRAINING AND SUPPORT

Ever heard that expression 'People leave managers, not organisations'? It's a quote in the book *First, Break all the Rules* by Marcus Buckingham, presenting the findings of Gallup research into what makes a great manager, and it is widely talked about in HR circles. I have no doubt that for many people, this was exactly the experience they felt they had when they made a decision to leave a job.

However, there are some that beg to differ. Research by Culture Amp suggests that a great manager makes little difference when they are in a 'bad' company. However, what they did find was that while good managers make a difference in a 'good' company, the quality of a leader makes a huge difference.[46]

---

46 www.cultureamp.com/blog/the-biggest-lie-in-hr-people-quit-managers.

I'm going to assume, because you are reading this book, that you are already a great leader who truly cares about creating the best company and employee experience. Of course, we can, and I believe should, always be working on our leadership skills. However, in this chapter we are focusing on how to help the managers on your team have a significant positive influence on the experience of the employees in their teams.

> In researching for this book, I spoke to a number of individuals about their personal experience working from home during the pandemic. One story really struck me. This person's work team went remote in March 2020 and it wasn't until August (five months later) they were asked the simple question: 'How is it going?' 'How are you going?'
>
> This was about 4.5 months too late for this employee.
>
> To put it into context; the manager didn't have a big team. Just two direct reports. Yet they failed in the most simple of tasks.
>
> This lack of attention left the employee feeling disconnected and undervalued. It left them looking for another job.

**Find a manager, not just a technician**

Most people are promoted for technical ability or years in the job. Rarely are they promoted simply because they are good at managing people. In fact, often management ability isn't even taken into account. And how can you get management experience before you are managing someone? You can't.

Taking a look at all of your existing managers, it is likely that most of them have never undergone any formal management training. It's likely been a lot of learning by experience, and learning (either consciously or not) from observing the actions of their own managers. This unfortunately can be good or bad depending on the calibre of the managers they've had.

To give your managers the best shot at doing a good job, and therefore the best chance of developing great mentoring relationships with their team members, it's a good idea to formalise some training.

A key starting point is for the managers to learn about themselves.

Go back to the personality tests I discussed in chapter 2. Choose a test that helps identify strengths and weaknesses as they apply to management ability. Ask your managers to do the test. As always, apply with caution. Make it clear they aren't being assessed on how well they do – it's not that kind of test. Rather the purpose is to help the manager work out where they might need support to develop and grow further into the role.

For people who aren't managers yet, depending on your company size, you could put in place something like a 'management track' where people who are identified with potential are given extra training, or allowed opportunities to 'act up' in higher roles for a time so they can get the hands-on experience. Whether this is possible or not, you still need a way to identify who these people with potential are, and it needs to be more than that they are good at the job they've been hired to do. We all know that just because someone is good at one thing, doesn't mean they will be good at something else. In fact, the opposite is often true. We all have strengths and weaknesses.

### Getting the relationship right

A manager's job is about more than just being a manager who is good at supervising the actual work being done, explaining how to do tasks correctly and making sure that the company isn't exposed to any risks from poor workmanship or mismanagement of client relationships. A manager is – whether they like it or not – a mentor as well. If an employee isn't getting the mentorship that they need, they'll go and find it somewhere else.

In order for a manager to be able to successfully mentor a team member they need a solid relationship. The strength of the relationship between the two individuals is the key determinant for how well a manager can do all the supervisory and team management tasks required of a manager.

When someone is working remotely, the relationship they have with their manager becomes even more important. That key supervisory relationship becomes an employee's main connection to the workplace. Without the buffer of other people around them in an office environment diluting any negativity, the bad aspects of a manager become even more obvious and harder to ignore. And that's when people leave.

## You do you, and I'll do me

For managers and employees to work well together, they need to have not just an understanding of the work that needs to be completed, but also how each person likes to work and what motivates them. By sharing their individual personality/strengths test results with each other they can get an insight into how each other thinks and works. They can then use that insight to collaboratively design a way of working with each other and avoid conflict from differing work styles. Teams don't work when everyone wants to do things their own way.

For example, some employees like to ask a lot of questions so might like to send lots of questions via Slack or email or whatever other tech is being used. This might make the manager feel like they are drowning and never getting their work done. The manager might prefer to have undisturbed time to focus, and so might ignore all the messages until one or two times a day and then answer them all at once. This situation could easily lead to the employee feeling annoyed at being ignored if they don't understand the manager's style.

If instead these two people can share straight up how they like to work, they can agree on a way that works for them both. Maybe letting the employee send all their messages to one place, and having agreed times when the employee knows the manager will respond. This avoids offense, discontent and anyone feeling like they are 'wrong' in the way they like to work. It's also a strong mark of respect for each other.

My good friend Lucy Dickens, author of *It's Time to do Law Differently*, has used the technique of creating 'User Manuals' at the law firm where she works. All of the team completed the Clifton Strengths Finder assessment, and then completed a one-page sheet answering questions like:
- kind of feedback I need and how to deliver it
- things I struggle with
- times/hours I like to work
- best ways to communicate with me.

After completing the User Manual all of the staff came together over a lunch to share and discuss their answers (where they felt comfortable to do so). The team then went away to fine tune their User Manual and then provided it to the people in their immediate work team as a way to guide their interactions at work.

I also read a great story about a manager who created a 'cheat sheet' for staff about working with him. When anyone new came along he'd give them a copy of the sheet and it gave them a big heads-up. He'd also often take feedback from the team on the sheet and update it as he learned more about himself or changed.

This kind of document is a great thing to add to your manager's toolkit. Even better if there is one for all staff. Just remember – you want everyone to buy into this sharing, not have it forced upon them. Requiring everyone to share what they might consider to be personal details won't bode well for creating the kind of trusting relationship you are aiming for.

## Training managers in how to manage

How your managers manage will have a big impact on the culture of your business and its success. Lots of management styles will get results – and might increase productivity and financial performance – but are they creating the culture you want? Don't leave it up to the managers. Train them how to manage in a way that suits your business goals.

Failing to train managers in how to manage is a key shortfall in many businesses. It's not good enough for managers to believe that glaring at someone (ever seen that episode of *Utopia*?) is enough to let them know something is wrong. It's not good enough when managers think that managing performance is something you call HR about, getting it out of their hands like a hot potato. You need to make your expectations clear and ensure they are met.

Do you want managers to have lots of feedback conversations? Do you want performance and conduct discussions to be shaped around alignment – or not – with company values and behaviours? Once you know how you want day-to-day management to look you can start to put in place a training regime.

One of my favourite things to do is get inside a business and work with companies to design training programs for managers. We don't just talk about all the legal risks like unfair dismissal claims and scare them with the costs to the business in terms of money, time and mental health. We don't just focus on giving them tips and strategies for holding difficult conversations.

Don't get me wrong. We talk about all of these things. But management training needs to be more than generic principles. We ask managers to participate in exercises to learn more about their own management style. We encourage them to role play a difficult conversation with one of their peers. We walk them through case examples so they can learn to spot the red flags. We focus on how the company wants managers to operate in their company in keeping with the company values and its policies and procedures. We provide ongoing coaching support. It's important that you give thought to what kind of managers you want and that you shape the training appropriately.

### Start with why – again

Before we get to any of that great training, there is a fundamental mindset shift that often needs to occur before managers will care about any of this. So we start by teaching the *why* behind managing performance and conduct. When people realise that failing to tell an employee what they are doing wrong means they don't know they need to improve, or how, and the likely outcome is the employee getting fired, they are much more open to managing their team. It's important for managers to learn that if you don't give someone feedback, you are denying them the right to improve and grow. Managers soon realise that they have the potential to help an employee change the course of their employment for the better. They have the chance to make a real difference.

After this, managers become much more receptive to management skills training. They ask more questions and are ready to absorb the tips and tricks. At this point we can start training them in the general principles, and the types of strategies to manage individual performance or conduct issues.

### Practise, test, review

Of course, good management training is much more than a really fun, informative and interactive workshop with someone like me. In order for skills to stay fresh, they need to be practised. It's not much good learning a skill one day and then never using it. Like me and golf lessons. Management isn't like riding a bike – it doesn't just come back to you when you need it. Managers need the opportunity to put their skills into use on a regular basis, and they too need to be assessed on how well they are managing.

Hold regular check-in meetings with your managers. Don't just talk about whether the team met its goals like sales targets or clients served. Ask about their team and how they are going managing them. Are they holding regular check-in sessions with all their team members? Do any team members have any issues that the manager would like to discuss in order to better manage them?

It's also important that the manager is not just self-assessing all the time. As we know, some people have wonderfully high opinions of themselves, but ask around and you might get a different view. So make sure you do that. Every now and then, check in with an individual in a manager's team to get a sense of how the team is working under that manager. Do they respect the manager? Love the manager? Think the manager needs to get a new job? 360-degree feedback is a wonderful tool.

It also doesn't have to be you doing all the asking all the time – or some kind of formal process. Encourage your managers to reach out to their own teams and ask them for feedback about their management style and how the team is functioning. It can be hard to hear criticism, but just as managers need to provide feedback to improve the people in their team, so too do managers need to hear feedback to improve management skills. And who better to hear it from than the people on the receiving end?

There's a lot of moving parts in creating a training regime for managers. Sometimes it's hard to remember all these things. Don't be afraid of creating a 'cheat sheet' or a 'toolkit' for your managers. This has the added advantage of being a way to make sure that expectations are clearly understood – a key component of any successful relationship. It's easy to have a conversation about things and come away with two different memories of what was said, a lot harder to do when the conversation is recorded in writing.

## Managing from afar

You might have realised that nothing I've said so far about training managers is specific to Homeforce teams. That's because the basic principles are all the same. But managing a team remotely requires an additional skill level. Virtual teams are by their nature much more autonomous and don't allow for a manager to constantly have an eye on everyone. How do you make sure that a manager is going to be capable in a virtual environment when they can't regularly see their team?

Some companies tried to fix that by trying to recreate an office environment online. During the COVID pandemic and the rush to set people up to work from home when social distancing measures were made law, some employers required everyone to be signed into a video meeting room for their whole working day. So they'd be at their desk working away with their video on so that anyone at any time could check that they were there and appeared to be working. I wonder what they did during a toilet break. Stuck a sign up on their desk? 'Left at 2:06, back in 5 minutes'?

Ultimately that requirement led to some really bad publicity for a number of companies. But that's not really the worst of it. Think about the effect that requirement probably had on those workers. They never got a minute of downtime. There was definitely no zoning out or staring off into the distance in that environment as you never knew who was watching.

Probably the worst effect of all? The destruction of trust. If you need to be able to see your staff working every minute of their allocated working hours, what does that say to your employees about how much you trust them to get on and do their job? It says a whole lot.

Without trust, your relationship is extremely limited. You will likely turn into a micro-manager. Any sense of autonomy that an employee might have felt they were gaining disappears. You are enforcing the 'us' versus 'them' mentality. Those workers won't bend over backwards for you, they won't go the extra mile. Rather they'll be out the door when the next best offer comes along.

Managers need to move beyond the mindset of, 'how do I know if they're working if I can't see them?' They need to embrace the autonomous nature of their workforce and rely on other methods to measure performance and productivity. They need to truly understand what their team are there to do – as agreed in their contracts and job descriptions. That is way more than making sure they have their bum on their seat for eight hours each day. Any good manager will be able to judge how well their people are working by their output anyway.

If managers aren't good at managing in an office environment, then they are highly unlikely to suddenly improve when working remotely. However, it's also not true that if someone is good at managing in an in-person environment they are going to be just as good managing remotely. How we manage needs to change.

## CHECK IN, NOT CHECK UP

It's been said that 'managing by walking around does not translate into managing by emailing around'.[47] I disagree with the implication in this statement that this is a bad thing. In my experience, a manager walking around meant someone checking up on you to make sure you were at your desk – not helpfully asking if you needed something. A person specifically emailing you or setting aside the

47 'The Implications of Working Without an Office', Ethan Bernstein, Hayley Blunden, Andrew Brodsky, Wonbin Sohn, and Ben Waber, *Harvard Business Review*, 15 July 2020 (hbr.org/2020/07/the-implications-of-working-without-an-office).

time to make a random call is, in my view, much more likely to be seen as a positive management action. We need to move from checking up to checking in.[48]

As Emma Walsh said during our interview, one of the most common things people put on their resumes is that they have great communication skills, and 'yet if we were all that good at it, honestly, there'd be world peace'. We all like to think we are great communicators, but it is often not the case – or at least not in all scenarios and with all people. It is refreshing how Emma acknowledges this and speaks about the need for people to be willing to think about whether their communication has landed and been understood the way intended. The need to do a lot of checking in.

It is true that it is a lot easier to manage when everyone is working in the same way, however that's unlikely to be the case. With over 40% of managers expressing low confidence about the ability to manage distributed teams, it is important to invest the time in your managers to improve their skills.[49] They will be a big part of the glue holding your distributed team together.

To provide support to managers who are managing distributed teams, some larger businesses are starting to implement new positions like a Director of Remote Work, or a Community Manager. The intention being that these people are specifically hired to ensure that distributed teams are functioning well, and that all people involved in the relationship are supported. Consider what additional resources you may need in your business to make the experience a success for managers and the whole team.

---

48 'Remote Managers are Having Trust Issues', Sharon K. Parker, Caroline Knight, & Anita Keller, 30 July 2020, *Harvard Business Review* (hbr.org/2020/07/remote-managers-are-having-trust-issues).

49 'Remote Managers are Having Trust Issues', Sharon K. Parker, Caroline Knight, & Anita Keller, 30 July 2020, *Harvard Business Review* (hbr.org/2020/07/remote-managers-are-having-trust-issues).

**Creating a great remote manager/employee relationship**

Whether you are having a relationship with someone who you see in the office every day, or someone who is in another country to you, the keys to a successful relationship remain the same. In my opinion it comes down to five things:

- trust
- respect
- shared expectations
- communication
- connection.

You don't need to be able to meet in person in order to have and maintain these things, but it is absolutely true that some of these things are easier to build in person because of the actions that happen incidentally when you see each other and share physical space.

You build trust in a relationship when you see the other person showing up to do their job each day, when you learn about their life incidentally as they arrive late one day and explain about traffic from their home location or because of trouble with getting their kids off to school.

You build respect in them as you listen in to their conversations with other employees and clients, as you see them reaching out to other employees to help with their workload or to explain something they don't understand.

Being in person, you can share expectations quickly because you can see and hear people working, and when you see something you don't like you can ask them to course correct.

Trust, respect and shared expectations are particularly important in a distributed team. While working in an office allows employees to keep their private life at home (if they choose to), that is much harder to do when working remotely. We see a window into someone else's life when there are video meetings and we see their home office space and how they've designed it, when their child slips into the room to just pass daddy a note, or whisper something into mummy's ear, or when we hear their partner or housemate in the background when on a telephone call. Giving these insights can make an employee feel very uncomfortable if they don't trust their manager and teammates.

Not only that, but it becomes necessary to talk about their personal lives as we ask them questions about their childcare arrangements and living arrangements to ensure that they have the necessary space and privacy at home to work remotely. It is super important that your employees feel they can trust you with their personal life.

The common thread in developing trust and respect and having shared expectations is good communication. It can be easier to communicate when you are a team sharing physical space because you see and walk past each other. You have the casual 'hello' and 'how was your weekend?' as you say good morning or meet each other in the kitchen. You can easily pop up from your desk and ask your colleague, 'Are you free? Can I have a minute?' You can pop out together and grab a coffee.

All of these incidental meetings and interactions with peers enable you to get to know each other, and with knowledge and familiarity comes trust and ultimately a sense of connection and belonging. Without this sense of connection to a common group and goal it can be very difficult for employees to feel part of a team and enable them to work together for a common goal. There is a valid fear that distributed teams will be less connected. But it doesn't have to be that way.

So how do we build these same feelings and sense of connection in a distributed team?

**Building good communication with your distributed team**

It's almost the standard response when people ask why a relationship broke down: 'We just didn't communicate very well. They didn't understand me. I couldn't get my point across.'

Being able to communicate well is key to ensuring that an employee is successful. The manager needs to be able to explain the requirements, the employee needs to be comfortable to ask questions when unsure, and they need to be able to work together to solve problems that arise. It's all about understanding and managing expectations.

But it's about more than just making sure an employee knows what they need to do. This should all be set out very clearly in those contracts of employment and job descriptions that you've already created. Managers need to go beyond that.

It's incredibly easy for an employee to start to feel alone and isolated when working from home, which if left unchecked can lead to mental health concerns. Without the ad hoc office interactions and communication and the ability to regularly see an employee in person in the office, you need to plan for other ways to keep a check on your employees and keep in touch with them. If you want to maintain the emotional and mental wellbeing of your staff, you need to put in place the right communication strategies. Strategies that the manager, team and individuals have agreed and committed to together.

## Choose a project management tool

There are hundreds of project management options. If you let it, choosing a project management tool can leave you seriously confused. Some of the more well known ones are Asana, Trello, Basecamp, Microsoft Flow and Monday. It doesn't matter which one you choose so long as it allows you to actively manage each project within the business in a way that everyone can see what is being done, by whom and when. Let me reiterate that. In a way that *everyone* can see what is being done, by whom and when.

This is a good thing for three reasons:

- Accountability is essential for a successful, productive team. Having an agreed outcome on a project management tool for the whole team or company to see will make most employees feel a sense of obligation and help keep them accountable to getting those tasks complete.

- Giving everyone the ability to see all company projects means that they are less likely to feel out of the loop. If they are curious about the progress of something they can go into the software and find out.

- It also means that managers are less likely to overload particular people when they can see a complete list of tasks assigned to that individual.

### Collaborate and listen

Ice is back . . . Sorry. Showing my age.

Any successful team requires collaboration. At first glance this seems pretty difficult to do when you are not sitting next to each other or at least within walking distance. However, if you dig a little deeper you will find it's not difficult at all – just different. Actually, in some cases it's not that different to what many people are doing when they do work next to each other or in the same building.

I'm talking about things like instant messaging, calling each other on the telephone (I'm sure if you've worked in an office building you've picked up the phone rather than walk up two flights of stairs), and having meetings.

Working in a distributed team, it can feel different to just pick up the phone. Employees may be less likely to do it when it isn't just an internal call. Whereas with instant messaging, it's possible that it can be overused and used for the wrong things. So the key here is to agree as a team what collaboration tools are going to be used, how and when. For example, maybe you use Teams chat or Slack and you create different channels for work matters and social chit chat.

Whatever you choose, make sure it works. Don't be afraid to adjust the rules as you go along. And do it regularly. Gallup research showed that for employees working 80% to 100% of the time remotely from the office, communications with a manager a few times each week led to 63% higher engagement, compared to only 48% when feedback is only provided a few times each month.[50]

Having said that – be aware of going overboard. It is natural and normal for employees to go long stretches without talking to one another. This is the deep work, get stuff done, period we are all always so desperate to zone into, and is often so hard to come by when working surrounded by other people. Good collaboration comes in bursts so figure out some good times to get 'busy together' and plan it in.[51]

### Asynchronous and synchronous communication

Communication can be asynchronous – when you communicate something to someone without expecting an immediate response (such as sending an email) or synchronous – when two or more people are exchanging information in real time.

---

50 'Performance Management must evolve to survive COVID-19', Ben Wigert and Heather Barrett, 31 August 2020 (www.gallup.com/workplace/318029/performance-management-evolve-survive-covid.aspx?utm_source=workplace_newsletter&utm_medium=email&utm_campaign=workplace_newsletter_dec_12292020&utm_content=takemoreagile_textlink_4&elqTrackId=d81bae0fb68f44c797db632cdffdafb3&elq=3354c170e31c45239507ccd205966fcb&elqaid=5655&elqat=1&elqCampaignId=1183).

51 'Successful Remote Teams Communicate in Bursts', Christopher Riedl and Anita Williams Woolley, 28 October 2020, *Harvard Business Review* (hbr.org/2020/10/successful-remote-teams-communicate-in-bursts?autocomplete=true).

A manager needs to become an expert at knowing which option is best for each kind of information that needs to be communicated. Sometimes you need a quick answer. Other times you might want to send some background information around to later discuss at a meeting – with no response required in the meantime. This is also known as 'flip learning' – send some information around to your people and have them read, watch or listen, and then come prepared with any questions and comments to a team meeting. This is a really useful style to embed learning and makes face-to-face time so much more efficient and productive.

Five years of managing remote teams has taught me that it is important to ensure that whatever communication strategies you have in place, the whole team is committed to them. There was nothing more rewarding for me than one of our quarterly meetings where we worked on our strategic plan, and when prompted by the facilitator to write down what is going well, the whole team wrote 'communication'.

We've achieved this by using a multitude of different communication tools. We use Teams video meetings for our twice weekly check-ins and any other ad hoc meetings we need, Teams chat function for quick questions where we are looking for more immediate responses, and email when we need to send documents and want someone to give some deeper consideration to our question. We are also not afraid to use the phone. This is often for debrief chats when one of us is driving home after a client meeting, or just when we don't feel like or need to have a video meeting.

The key to all of these tools is choosing the right one at the right time - and making sure everyone does the same thing.

**Meetings**

Meetings on the other hand, are by their nature much more complex. In an office environment it is really common for meetings to happen spontaneously, often without a huge amount of thought as to who should be present. With a distributed team it will work a lot better if they are planned in advance as much as possible.

### What meetings?

What meetings do you normally have in your office? Are there some that are regularly scheduled on a daily, weekly, monthly or some other basis? What about the other kinds of meetings that are arranged on an as needed basis around workflow or directions for different tasks? How are these organised?

Whatever regular meetings you would normally have, you need to plan for these to continue when people work remotely. If you have a daily huddle where you all share what you are working on for the day, you need to move that to an online forum.

### Where and when?

Consider your options. Do you want people to attend the daily huddle via video conference? Or is a telephone hookup sufficient? If you are transitioning to a Homeforce or have a hybrid workforce where some people are in the office some of the time, then you need to think about how everyone feels attending that meeting.

My worst experiences during video conferences have been where most everyone in the meeting is in the same room, and it's only me and perhaps a few other people who are using video conferencing. It's awkward. You can't always hear everything due to rustling papers and other background noise. You know that people are having side conversations but you can't hear them. Sometimes you can't see all the in-person participants and no one lets you know who is present.

There is always this feeling that you are missing something, don't really know what is going on, and the people in the room and what they have to say are more important than those on video.

Instead of this unbalanced approach – why not ask everyone to attend the meeting via video or telephone? It gets rid of that awkward feeling, puts everyone on an even playing field, and prevents the feeling of a two-level hierarchy.

An added bonus is that it saves business time. I don't know about you, but my experience of internal office meetings is often a feeling that a 10 a.m. meeting time means people start walking in the door at 10 a.m. Or even worse they come in at 10 a.m. and start making themselves a cup of tea. With a video conference there is definitely no need to wait for people in the office to walk into the meeting room. It is much easier to enforce start times and get things underway on time.

Another consideration is the timing of meetings. As your Homeforce expands you may find that you take on people from different time zones. If so – how are you going to handle that? Have multiple meetings? Or perhaps you will just ask everyone to share their daily tasks in a written format? One of the keys to any communication strategy is going to be the ability to adapt to changing circumstances. You will need to consider each of the people who need to attend the meeting and adapt to their circumstances – within reason of course.

## Plan it out

Once you've worked out what meetings you need, plan the agenda. Having a baseline starting point with some key categories for discussion points will make the meetings flow more easily as everyone is used to the format and knows where to add their topics. Don't forget to make one of those points a bit of time for some general chit chat. What did you do on the weekend? How is your daughter who was sick? I'm reading this great book lately and just had to tell you ... Business is definitely not business, business, business all the time. It's important to make sure you add some time for relationship building.

For each meeting plan, don't forget to consider if any part of the meeting is simply passing on information. Can it be shared asynchronously before the meeting to save time? Same goes if you are seeking the opinions of your attendees for something. Ask them to consider the question and brainstorm their answer privately before the meeting starts. This will create more diversity of opinion and solutions – rather than the group think that can happen in meetings.

## Plan in some chit chat

Speaking of relationship building, once you've programmed your essential work-related meetings – don't stop there. We've already worked out that there is certain ad hoc communication that occurs in an office. You can't just give all of that up. Now some of you may be thinking giving up all of that ad hoc conversation time in the kitchen and standing around having morning tea is a benefit of having a Homeforce. Surely if they aren't doing that, they will be doing more work and being more productive? The answer is – that depends.

For some people that may well be the case. Think about all those part-time workers who have commitments after work, like elite sport training. Talk about get in, head down and work done so they can get out. For others, they may need that downtime from work in order to start again more focused. If that's the case, they will need to have a break in some form or other. Also – the benefit of that kind of employee interaction as a break is that there is a sharing of knowledge that happens about company matters (not just gossip), and it is building bonds between team members.

Rather than cutting it out increasing productivity, the fact is that ensuring you have that non work-related communication means that your employees will work better as a team and that leads to productivity gains.

So encourage teams to schedule meetings where there is no specific agenda other than checking in with each other, talking about the weekend, asking any random questions that might have arisen, seeing if they need anything, and so on. Unless you schedule time for those non-work meetings, employees might feel like they are disturbing you or their manager or might just never get up the confidence to ask. It also allows a manager to spot potential opportunities for training.

### To video or not to video?

Early in the pandemic the shares for Zoom went through the roof as a significant number of businesses tried to replicate their in-person meetings using video conferencing. But just because you are having a meeting doesn't mean it has to be using video. Have you heard about 'Zoom fatigue'? It's one of those new expressions we are so familiar with as a result of COVID-19. To start with, everyone rejoiced at still being able to 'see' each other, but then pretty quickly, everyone was joining meetings with their video off.

Why? Because being on a video screen is a lot different to being one of a crowd in a meeting room. When you are on screen you are in close up and everyone is looking directly at you – or might be. You can't just zone out and look off into the distance. Whenever you aren't focused people assume you are reading your emails or surfing the web. There is a real need to be 'on'.

Make your decision to use video a conscious choice – not just the default option. It might not be necessary for all meetings. Some research has found that audio-only calls can be better for collaboration as they promote equality in speaking time, which means a potential greater sharing of ideas.[52] It's also been found that we are better at reading emotions in voice only calls.[53] This might have something to do with paying more attention to what we are listening to and less to how we look.

If you are using video, agree on some ground rules. Perhaps it is a team decision that all meetings will be with video on. Make sure everyone knows to be on mute when they join and to stay on mute. We've no doubt all experienced someone who forgot and shared a personal conversation with their team, or was yelling at their kids, or singing along to a radio in the background. The most embarrassing audio faux pas I heard was someone who was part of a teleconference with a Court and put the call on hold – only for the Court and all other participants to be required to listen to their horrible hold music the entire time, and severely limiting the ability for people to be heard over the music.

And don't forget to make it interesting. Teach your managers how to be online facilitators. There is nothing more draining than having to sit in an online meeting just listening to someone talking monotonously.

Teach them facilitation skills using games and engagement strategies to keep everyone connected and involved. Most video conferencing facilities like Zoom have functions like a chat box, emojis you can use on screen to express how you feel about what someone is saying, break-out rooms, and different screen views and the option to share screens. There are some amazing tools online and having managers skilled in using them will make the world of difference – not just in how they connect with their team, but also with your clients.

52 'Successful Remote Teams Communicate in Bursts', Christopher Riedl and Anita Williams Woolley, 28 October 2020, *Harvard Business Review* (hbr.org/2020/10/successful-remote-teams-communicate-in-bursts?autocomplete=true).

53 Kraus (2017) 'Voice-only communication enhances empathic accuracy', *American Psychologist*.

## Document everything

Whatever meeting you have, make sure you document it. This might feel a little over the top – and it definitely could be taken over the top – however it is really important that key information and decisions from meetings are recorded. This way people who couldn't be present, or didn't need to be present but are affected by the decision, can read what occurred and avoid feeling 'out of the loop'.

## Make it fun

Finally, don't forget to inject some fun. If people are just turning up and getting directions and moving on, the meetings will get stale and boring. This might be necessary sometimes – quick meetings where there is some urgency to the work that needs to be done – but it isn't necessary all the time. And no one wants to be part of meetings like that all the time. Start by asking everyone to pull those cards out of the onboarding box you sent them. Showing a thumbs up sign during a video meeting gets a little more interesting than watching a bunch of heads nodding up and down. Make sure you use them yourself too – it's always about leading by example.

Once you've mastered that, get creative. Inject some fun into meetings. One law firm I know in Perth did just that during the height of the coronavirus lockdown. They asked everyone to wear their funniest hat to a video meeting. Extra points (laughs) awarded if you made it yourself. Perhaps you could do something similar but send everyone a box of craft supplies beforehand. Give everyone the same supplies and see what they come up with.

Even if you don't have a budget for these kind of activities, something is better than nothing. It might just be asking everyone to share a fun fact about their week at the regular team meeting. Perhaps a story about the latest crazy thing their child or dog had done. Dress ups are always good – favourite footy team, pyjamas, a certain colour. Or maybe pulling out the quiz from the weekend paper and asking the whole team to sit around and puzzle it out together.

You can always get a little personal too. Ask different people to give a tour of their workspace, or their home. Maybe 'bring your pet to work day' online. Or perhaps to share something about themselves that would be obvious to everyone if they worked in an office together. For example, how tall they are.

All of these activities have one thing in common. They are about fostering communication and building trusted relationships between team members. We need to learn about each other to develop the level of trust required for a team to function at optimum levels.

## OTHER HYBRID MEETING TIPS

There is no doubt that hybrid meetings are going to be a thing of the future. Although I touched on some tips above with my recommendation that all attendees be separately logged in (whether they are in the office or distributed), this might not always be possible, or preferable. In that case, where you have some people sharing a room and others logged in separately from various locations, I suggest the following strategies:

- Have someone in the office nominated to monitor the people who are logged in online. When you don't want to seem rude by calling out — or perhaps you can't be heard properly when you do — there is nothing worse than sitting online typing a question in the chat or waving your arm around like crazy and not getting a response. Having a nominated person checking the chat box regularly is helpful to ensure continued engagement of those online.

- Make sure everyone in the office and online knows who is participating. This is just simple courtesy.

- Make sure the people in the office can see the faces of all those who have logged in online, rather than it just being the meeting coordinator with their laptop in front of them. This will help those in the office remember to allow time for their online colleagues to speak and participate.

- Have a camera set up on the office so that all people who are in attendance are visible to those online. This should also help to limit any natural inclination of people in the office to whisper to their neighbour.

- Make sure the purpose of the meeting is clear and that timekeeping is exceptional. This should always be the case with any meeting but is particularly important when you are trying to manage hybrid dynamics.

### An open (virtual) door policy

For some there is no doubt the fear, and likely the reality, that if you schedule a meeting just to 'check in' that the employee may just say, 'I'm fine'. This happens enough and everyone will start to view these meetings as a waste of time and slowly they disappear off everybody's schedule.

I've explained above why that's so important to avoid. But there are also other means to continue communication and form that team bond.

A common occurrence in the office environment is the person turning to the neighbour next to them and just starting up a conversation with, 'Hey, have you done this before? Can you help . . .' Or the team member who gets up, knocks on the manager's open door and says, 'Hey, have you got a minute?' Depending on who the manager is and how they like to work they might find that most of their day is spent answering these quick questions, helping their team members move forward.

This is what's known as an 'open door policy'. If a team is used to working this way and it makes them effective then it's important to try to replicate it in the Homeforce world. How? Technology, of course.

It could be as simple as telling people to just pick up the phone. Depending on the size of your existing office this might be a common thing. I remember when I worked in a business with three levels it was pretty common to just dial someone internally rather than take the stairs or elevators. Of course, eventually I realised taking the stairs each time I needed to talk to someone was a good idea. You get the picture, I'm sure.

Although we all love our smartphones these days (well, except for my husband), many of us have an aversion to actually calling people on them. This is especially so amongst the millennials. Research shows 75% would rather text than call.[54] So don't worry about making them call anyone; go with natural instinct.

They can achieve the same effect of saying, 'Have you got a minute?' by sending a text or voice message. There are loads of different apps that can do this: the standard message app on your phone, or other specialised team communication apps like Slack, Teams and Voxer. Some organisations even use Facebook groups and messenger to communicate. Encouraging voice messages is a great idea as they allow people to get their message across more quickly (most people can talk faster than they type), and it also brings added connection when team members hear each other's voices.

## Team building

Don't get turned off here and think I'm going to start talking about wildlife survival adventure camps, or trust exercises like falling back into the hands of your team members. These kinds of things

---

54 www.openmarket.com/press/study-millennials-would-rather-text-than-talk-infographic/.

were big back in the 1980s, and have come back with a vengeance because of people like Bear Grylls, but they have definitely made a lot of Baby Boomers and Gen Xers a bit dismissive of the phrase 'team building activities'.

The reason the phrase keeps hanging around though, and why companies keep sending staff on these things, is because they really can work. Now if your team is totally dysfunctional it's going to need more than a few trust exercises to bring them back together. But if you use these activities at the right time, and regularly, they can stop a team from falling apart.

When you have a distributed team working remotely you need to get creative. Just like the regular video meetings, think about how you can schedule some meetings which are specifically for team building.

One law firm – Law Squared – got creative during the coronavirus pandemic restrictions in order to keep up team connection. They sent all their staff a portrait drawn on a canvas and a bunch of paints. At the next meeting everyone was asked to sit around painting together while they received instructions from a professional artist. The kicker? All the portraits were of different team members – so everyone was painting the face of someone else in the business. Not only did this activity inspire everyone's creativity and give them some fun time, it also created some team bonds.

A good friend of mine runs a law firm in Perth called Blackwall Legal. When the pandemic struck Perth in March 2020 he acted quickly to develop a plan, send his staff home and keep the business moving.

In order to keep the team relationships going he established a daily check-in meeting for anyone who was working that day.

You are probably thinking they all sat around, said good morning and then shared their to-do list. Now there probably was some of that, but what I loved about his story was that the first thing they did was the daily quiz in *The West Australian*. They pooled their collective brain power - quite considerable - and tried to beat two out of ten on the quiz.

The purpose of this? Being able to see each other and know they aren't alone even though they are physically, getting together to work on something as a team, and a bit of light relief. Everything you need to build relationships and keep mental health positive.

Now if you have the budget, one of the best things you can do is get everyone together in person. 'What?' I hear you ask. Isn't this whole book designed to tell business owners that they don't need to have their teams together and that a Homeforce can be as effective as an office environment? Well – yes, it is designed to do that. And I truly believe in that premise.

Yet as I've said earlier, the success of your business will often come down to your team – their skills as individuals and, importantly, how they function together. As I've said earlier, it can be easier to form a bond in person than it is by writing letters, or talking on the phone or using video.

So set some budget aside and think about bringing your team together in person. Law Squared, mentioned earlier, is a good example of this. They are a distributed team based in three different offices in Sydney, Melbourne and Brisbane, Australia. Prior to the pandemic, each quarter they would bring all of their team members together in one of those cities. They mixed it up so that not everyone was travelling all the time. Given the short distance between the cities it is easy to get together for a couple of days and only one overnight. This gives them a chance to strengthen their team bonds.

If this seems completely out of your reach – perhaps your team are distributed around the world – then make it a team goal. Work out what kind of a budget you need to pay for everyone's flights, accommodation and living expenses while there, and tell the team. Let them know how much extra revenue the company needs to bring in to achieve this goal. Gamify it.

One business I know, Webinar Ninja, was in exactly this situation. The owners are based in Sydney but their team is spread around the world. In 2019 they brought their goal to life and were able to bring all of their team together in Bali, Indonesia. In an interview with co-owner Nicole Baldinu, she described the retreat as an incredible event and definitely a worthwhile investment providing an opportunity for most of the team to meet and work together in person for the first time.

Nicole mostly valued the ability to collaborate, sharing that as the different operational teams worked together in person 'they got to see a different perspective. They got to see the way everyone contributes in a different way to the team and brings their own skillset.' But equally as valuable seems to have been the non-work time. Nicole said, 'It was fun. We made memories together' and that it has continued to be 'impactful' as she hears her team constantly referring to the retreat when new teammates join.

This retreat was a clear example of creating a moment that matters in a work relationship.

**Surprise and delight**

If you are into marketing tactics then you've probably heard the phrase 'surprise and delight' before. It is a super valuable concept when marketing to clients and can make a big difference to the success of marketing initiatives. However, it doesn't have to be limited to use with clients.

Remember earlier I suggested focusing on the employee experience when you plan your onboarding process? Well – don't stop there. Once a business has its employees it is really easy to slip into the comfortable feeling of believing that you don't need to do any more for them. I mean you are paying them a good wage and perhaps a few extra things in exchange for the work they are doing, right? What more could they ask for?

Psychology tells us that humans want to be rewarded and recognised. People want to be thought about – in a good way of course. It can be easy to feel alone and separate in a little home office, but if that person knows someone is thinking of them and has their welfare at heart, it can totally change the experience.

I've given a few surprise and delight examples already. The box of craft supplies prior to a meeting, painting portraits. It can be much simpler than that too. Maybe a tea bag and a biscuit arriving just in time for a scheduled morning tea time meeting. Some great ideas and examples we can use came out of the pandemic. One law firm sent a letter to employees who were in lockdown attaching an Uber eats voucher. Maybe you want to send flowers to brighten up an employee's home office.

As usual, it doesn't have to cost you a lot of money. And don't fall into the trap of making it regular – hardly a surprise then is it? It could be as simple as a card with a message of thanks, or a funny note to make them laugh. Maybe you send your employees some supplies so that they can send some notes to their teammates.

Don't think it needs to be the same for everyone too. Generic company-branded merchandise – mugs, pens, caps or shirts – have their place, but sometimes something extra is called for. The more personal you can make it the more valued and pleased the employee will feel. The employee who loves gardening who gets some bulb packets in the mail. The employee who loves their dog and gets a chew toy for them. The employee who loves running and gets a new pair of ear buds to block out the road noise and listen to their favourite music or podcast.

Take a little time out of your week to surprise and delight your employees and you will not only make them feel good, they may also start talking about your business with others, and most importantly, you will have their loyalty. Loyal employees are more likely to hang around, lowering your turnover costs and creating a more bonded team.

## Accountability groups

As I said earlier, one of the key elements of a high-performing team is accountability. Although asking people to turn their video on all day for monitoring purposes has got an understandably bad rap, it isn't all bad. I know many teams who are self-selecting to have their video conference on all day so they feel they are all there working together. Or at the very least they are implementing specific virtual co-working sessions. It might be for a specific group, or just for anyone who wants to join in.

Sometimes it's agreed everyone's microphone is on the whole time so that the usual sounds of working with a team are experienced and a quick, 'Hey can you help?' gets answered straight away. Maybe it's set up to play some easy listening music. Other times it might be quiet with you all on mute and just asking a question when you need to. If the conversation starts to get a bit too deep the involved people can just breakaway into a separate breakout room.

Other ways to encourage accountability that isn't so in your face is to have daily check ins. Whether a quick 10-minute video chat, or just a round robin of what you've accomplished on instant messaging, it's all still a way to hold yourself and your team accountable to achieving the results you want.

## Be consistent – yet open to change

Whatever process and tools are chosen to be used for communication, it is important to be consistent. Don't tell people to use instant messaging for personal comments and then send an email yourself. Don't require everyone to have their video on for meetings and then make an excuse for yourself. Don't tell your team that everyone, whether office based or not, needs to attend meetings via video and then end up in a meeting room with a bunch of people in the office.

Create a plan and follow it. That doesn't mean it can't change if things aren't working. If something is not working – call it out and consciously come up with a new plan, rather than just falling back on old habits.

\* \* \*

To ensure business success you can't just leave it all to chance hoping that the managers know how to manage, and the employees will get on and do their jobs. You need to set them up for success. You need to be ready and willing to create systems and processes to ensure that relationships are built and developed over time.

## Step 5 summary

- Focus on the individual and set them up for success.

- Create and execute a purpose-built induction program that effectively communicates the overall business expectations.

- Hold whole-company or cross-team social interactions to encourage building of relationships across teams.

- Train employees on how to work remotely. Don't just give them a laptop and assume they can work the same way at home.

- Hire the right managers.

- Encourage team members to share their 'User Manual' and develop good communication protocols.

- Train managers on how to manage in a remote work and hybrid setting.

- Put real effort into understanding the purpose of meetings and making them functional and fun.

# CHAPTER 9

# Step 6: Evaluate the result

'Great things in business are never done by one person. They're done by a team of people.'

Steve Jobs

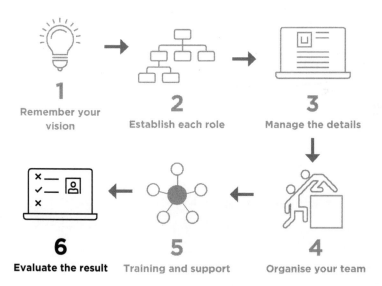

**1**
Remember your vision

**2**
Establish each role

**3**
Manage the details

**6**
Evaluate the result

**5**
Training and support

**4**
Organise your team

By picking up this book you are committing to seriously considering, if you haven't already started, building a Homeforce. One of the first things I asked you to do was to create a vision. What did you want your Homeforce to look like? What impact did you want it to have on your business? Was it all about financial goals? Was it about bringing flexibility to your workforce? Was it about wanting to reach the best talent around the world? Whatever it was – these or other things – it is personal to you and specific to your business. Not anyone else's.

Step 6 in the Homeforce REMOTE Framework is to assess whether or not you've reached 'success'.

So how do you do that? Is it just a feeling? When will you know if you've reached it? If you've been in business for any length of time then you will know it is very easy to never feel like you've reached success. There might be momentary celebrations, and then you are already moving on to the next thing on the list. Especially with something like implementing a Homeforce. So many of the requirements for success are ongoing and it is a constant moving feast.

## WHAT GETS MEASURED GETS MANAGED

Whoever said that knew what they were talking about. (It was Peter Drucker – legendary management consultant.) In order for you to feel a sense of achievement, you need to know if you've reached the vision goals you set for yourself. The only way to do that is to measure them.

### Measure what, and how, and when?

So let's talk about measuring. What can we measure, and how? The accountants like this one and talk about it a lot. It usually results in printing out lots of financial reports. However, your goals for a Homeforce more than likely went a lot further than financial.

This is where you need to go back to the vision you created for yourself in Step 1. Pull out that mind map, vision board, vision story, journal entry or whatever it was that you created to describe your vision for your Homeforce. What did you identify as being your reasons for creating a Homeforce? What were your markers of success? It's now time to take each one and work out a measurement so that you can continually track your progress.

Your vision of success more than likely included benefits to your employees, clients, overall business and you personally. The questions I asked you to consider when formulating your vision included something like these:

- Is your goal to still have an office?

- If you have one, is it significantly smaller with most employees just hot desking from time to time? Or is the whole purpose of it just for client meetings and internal business meetings?

- Has your business grown financially? Or maybe it was just more about cutting costs, reducing office expenses such as rent, phones and computers. Or perhaps salaries are down as you offer a point of difference that is more valuable to employees than money?

- How are clients being serviced? Is all interaction online? Are you providing a 'we come to you' service?

- How many employees? Are they scattered around the world? Are there any physical meetings? How are they interacting with each other, with you and with clients? Is employee turnover down? Are they happier? Is employee engagement up? Have you introduced greater workplace flexibility around hours of work?

- How does your personal life look now? Are you working fewer hours? Are you spending more time at work doing the things you enjoy? Are you happier?

## MEASURING SUCCESS

### Financial reports

Let's start with the easy ones. If you've got a great online bookkeeping system then you have at your fingertips the ability to produce a range of financial reports with a few clicks. If you have a great bookkeeper or accountant they can also probably customise something that's specific to your goals.

The key measurements that you are likely to be looking for in your financial statements are revenue and expenses. Revenue appears to be a simple equation – has it increased, stayed the same or decreased since starting the Homeforce?

However, nothing is that simple. You will need to look at revenue before Homeforce, and revenue after Homeforce, and it will be necessary to consider the different points along your transformation journey. It will also be necessary to compare it not just to the previous month or quarter, but to an appropriate comparison, like the previous financial year. For example, your monthly revenue six months after starting the Homeforce might be lower than before you started the Homeforce, and it might be lower than the same period last financial year. However, perhaps when you look at the figures you can see that there was a big dip month and that revenue has been steadily increasing since.

Also, as with anything else, revenue is affected by many things. It may be that the big dip was caused by losing a big client that went into liquidation. Clearly nothing to do with your Homeforce. Or maybe there was a big increase in revenue because a new client that you had won via tender started to use your services. Again, nothing to do with your Homeforce if the tender was won before it started. You need to ensure that you have considered all of those variables before determining to what extent the Homeforce has impacted revenue.

Now let's turn to expenses. Again this might seem like an easy equation. Are expenses down, the same or higher since Homeforce implementation? However, I suggest that you get a little more specific about what you are measuring. Depending on what you decided to measure, you need to make sure that those specific measurements have been separately accounted for in your financials.

Rent will be an obvious one. Other items might be office expenses like computers, internet usage, telephone systems and stationery supplies. Maybe you were paying for staff meals or taxis home if they worked late into the night. Take a detailed look into all of your expense categories. Go beyond the overall titles and consider whether anything caught within them will fall into the bucket of being no longer required with a Homeforce.

When you are doing your review, you will clearly be able to see if expenses are down in the categories you have identified. If they aren't – for example, you are still paying the same for an internet service and you have an office half the size – it leads to some obvious questions.

It's worthwhile sitting down with your bookkeeper or accountant to let them know about your plans for a Homeforce in the early days of the plan. Tell them your goals and work with them to identify what you can track in your financials, what needs to be adjusted to get a proper measurement, and to make sure that they are providing you with the reports you need when you need them.

### Create an audit checklist

For some things I recommend a good old checklist. These are the things that you can just ask yourself and tick *yes* or *no*. For example, do you have the office you wanted? For some of you that might be no office at all – so write that on the checklist – 'Am I still using a physical office?' Leave some room to write comments too. Maybe you still have an office but you've reduced your office capacity by 80%. This kind of analysis will show whether you are on track.

You'll also notice as you are preparing this checklist that some of these items will require other people in your business to be measuring things on a daily, weekly or other basis. For example, when it comes to clients, maybe one of your goals was to change how you are servicing them, such as moving from in-person meetings to all online. It's going to be very hard to ask employees to remember after a long period of time how many in-person meetings they did compared to online. So how are they going to track that?

Another item in the client category might be numbers of new clients and turnover of all clients. Again, this is a situation where you might also be wanting to gather data along the way. How did those clients find you and why did they decide to do business with you? Was it because of your profile as a Homeforce business? What about the clients that left? Why did they leave? Did it have anything to do with moving to a Homeforce? These kinds of questions should be part of your normal onboarding process, and feedback process. Keep track of this information somewhere so that it's ready at your fingertips when you are doing your Homeforce review.

On the employee side I'd be asking the question, 'Where are my employees located?' You might want to list a total number of employees, with percentages who are still in the office, at home, or perhaps in a co-working space. If employee retention and reduction in turnover was a goal for you, add that to your audit list too. How many employees have resigned since the Homeforce plan started? Why did they leave? Make sure your exit process is asking that question.

Finally, assess how the Homeforce has impacted your life. What were the personal goals that you had? If a goal was to be working fewer hours then the best way to track this is with daily timesheets. You don't need to follow that six-minute unit that so many lawyers use. A good half-hour block should be sufficient. Create some categories that you want to measure and apply them. For example, client work, business development, business admin. You might even want to track some of your personal time too. Have you been spending your free time doing what you wanted? Exercise, family time, hobbies, reading?

Creating this checklist will make things serious. You are truly committing to doing what needs doing to achieve these results.

Because who wants to make a big change and come up short? Don't just keep your goals to yourself, either. Let your team know so that they can feel that much more connected to your purpose and so they can help you measure what needs measuring on an ongoing basis.

## Use engagement surveys

### Staff engagement

Chances are if you've ever worked in a large organisation you've been asked to complete an engagement survey at some point or another. HR departments and change consultants love to use them. Depending on where you worked the attitude towards them might have been negative: 'This is such a waste of time.' Or maybe: 'What does it matter? They won't do anything anyway.' Or maybe it was positive: 'It is so good to be able to say how I feel anonymously.'

All of your staff will approach this with their own views about such surveys. In this situation, we are using an engagement survey to get an understanding of how the change to a Homeforce has impacted staff.

In order to do that, you need a starting point. So the first time you do an engagement survey needs to be before you've even started the transition to a Homeforce. Potentially before you've even told them about your plans. Your first survey will tell you how things really are now.

You can grab an off-the-shelf engagement survey, and there are some fabulous ones available. However, given you have such a clear goal in mind, you may want to tailor the questions, or add some questions, to ensure that you are measuring the things you want to measure and not just general satisfaction (or lack of it) at work.

Don't forget to include some open-ended questions in the survey to encourage the responders to make comment on what is going well and what they think can be done better. There is no better source for continuous improvement than suggestions from the people who are directly impacted and living the experience daily.

Once you have a starting point, you know where things can be improved. In some cases, you might get great results in your initial survey and you are just looking to maintain that. I suggest that you repeat the survey – exactly the same – at six months and then twelve months after the Homeforce implementation plan starts. You might see a dip at six months as everyone adjusts to the changes, but hopefully by twelve months you will be starting to see the improvements you were looking for.

The benefits of using staff feedback to measure and improve working arrangements can't be overstated.

Deloitte UK recently used a staff survey to help it determine the structure of its new Deloitte Works program. With over 15,000 responses, they found that over 90% answered that 'choice' and 'flexibility' should be at the heart of how they work in the future. This feedback led to a decision, in contrast to many other similar organisations, not to set a specific number of days that staff are required to be in the office. 'Instead,' writes Richard Houston, Senior Partner and Chief Executive at Deloitte North and South Europe and Deloitte UK, in a recent LinkedIn article, 'our people can choose how often they come to the office, if they choose to do so at all, while focusing on how we can best serve our clients.'[55]

The article goes on to make it clear that this is not a set-and-forget program. Deloitte plan to 'trial' new ways of working and use feedback from those trials to shape the firm's working arrangements in the years to come.

---

55 'Adapting to the future of work' by Richard Houston (www.linkedin.com/pulse/adapting-future-work-richard-houston/), 18 June 2021.

## Client engagement

Let's not forget the clients. Without them we don't have a business. It's no good implementing a Homeforce and having super-happy employees if the clients are leaving in droves. So let's measure their engagement and satisfaction too. Some of this data will be collected via onboarding and exit interviews we mentioned earlier, but it's a good idea to measure overall satisfaction from time to time.

Again – the first time to do this is before you start implementing any changes towards a Homeforce. You want to know exactly how they feel about your business, its products and services, before you start making changes. Then measure again in about twelve months. Any earlier and you might start to be annoying.

You don't just need to stop at a survey. You could also ask particular clients if they will participate in interviews so that you can delve deeper into some of the topics being covered in the survey.

The key with any data collection is to make sure that you aren't just collecting it. You need to review and analyse the data and work out what changes you can make to improve the overall outcomes and experience of your clients.

## DON'T LEAVE IT TOO LONG

The measurement tasks and tools suggested above are generally longer term tools. However, it isn't a good idea to let change management happen for too long without more regular review. Sometimes it is just too late to try to measure something after six months because you might have lost the opportunity to fix whatever may have gone wrong.

You might like to take a leaf out of Emma Walsh's book and try something like a 'Reflection Friday'. Every week or two she takes the time to reflect with a colleague over questions like:

- Is the team okay?

- What do we need to do more of and less of?

- Did the work priorities we had work for us?

- How are we feeling at the end of this week?

I suggest that you develop your own set of questions that you can reflect on each week or fortnight in relation to your Homeforce change process. Don't make them all practical assessments of tasks completed or not. Remember to focus on the feelings and to reflect on your vision to see if you are achieving the impact you want.

## DON'T LOSE THE FOREST FOR THE TREES

What gets measured gets managed. We've just worked out there is truth in this statement. However, a word of caution: there is the possibility that too much focus on one thing means that other important things will get missed. That's why it's important every now and then to reassess why you are measuring what you are measuring. Is it still the right thing to be measuring? Is it actually helping you determine if the business is successful and moving in the direction that you want it to be going?

Don't let your measurements just become a habit. Build in the time to do a review of the metrics you are using, and consult with others about whether they are still the ones you need to be focusing on. If not – change them up.

## Step 6 summary

- Get clear on the metrics you are going to be measuring to determine success. This will likely include benefits to your employees, clients, overall business and you personally.

- Create the financial reports, checklists and engagement surveys you need to adequately measure those metrics.

- Schedule a time to review the metrics and make sure they remain relevant.

PART III

# Bringing it all together

# CHAPTER 10

# You must make this a priority

'Be not afraid of growing slowly, be afraid only of standing still.'
Chinese Proverb

Is creating a Homeforce going to be easy? Probably not. Is it going to be worth it? Absolutely – if you do it right. But if you truly want to create a Homeforce that has a positive impact on your business, your team and your life then you have to believe in it yourself.

Knowing and wanting all the positive effects that can come from a Homeforce is not enough. You need to make this change a priority. You need to allocate the time, get the right people, and be prepared to spend some money to make it a reality. More than anything, you need to stay true to your vision.

## TIME AND MONEY

Ever heard that expression, 'you can spend the time or the money'? In building circles my husband uses the phrase: 'Choose two: Time, money or quality. You can't have all three.' So if you want quality – it's either going to take time, or money.

It's usually the case that there is the ability to speed up a process by spending some money. For example, you might choose to outsource creation of the employment documents, job descriptions,

Homeforce policy and the like. You might hire a consultant to create and conduct the engagement surveys. You could spend the time doing all of these things yourself – but it will be a lot faster to engage an expert. It will just cost you some money.

There are some things you can't outsource though. Creating your vision for a Homeforce is one such obvious thing. The issue often overlooked when in a hurry is the need for you to be the leader of this process. It is your vision, after all. Your team and your clients want to know that you are leading this change and that it is all under control. They don't want to see it handed off to some consultant that they've never heard of and don't have a personal relationship with.

Make sure you spend your time and money in the right places and with the right people.

## RIGHT PEOPLE

Speaking of right people, it's true to say that success comes easier if we have the right people around us. For you, this might mean a people specialist like me to help you plan the process, document the changes and provide constant support for you and your managers with any questions that arise during the workplace change process. It probably also means the right finance person – your CFO, bookkeeper or accountant.

You might also like to consider finding a mentor. Someone who's been there, like me, who can answer your questions, empathise with the challenges and encourage you with their own positive story.

Or maybe you just need someone who is your number one supporter no matter what you are doing. A husband, wife, best friend or even a counsellor, who provides unqualified support but has the ability to make sure you are looking after yourself and isn't afraid to ask you some hard questions from time to time.

Handpick your team with care as you will be working with them for quite some time and they will have a big say in whether you succeed. You need people who are skilled, experienced and have your back.

## STAY TRUE

There will absolutely be times that you doubt yourself. Change is never easy, even when we want it. Clients might rebel, employees may struggle, and you might get frustrated trying to adjust to this new way of doing business. Don't let your fears or the difficulties get in the way of pursuing your goal. Keep that vision board front and centre. Put it on the wall. Bring out your vision plan every day or week to remind yourself of your goal and your *why*. Make sure that your support team know about it and can help you come back to centre whenever things go astray.

There is a reason you chose to pick up this book. Don't forget it.

# What happens from here?

'To love what you do and feel like it matters, how could anything
be more fun?'
Katharine Graham

## THE FUTURE OF WORK

The year 2020 brought a great flood of change to the world of work. What had been a slowly building transformation was forced to speed up to respond to a worldwide crisis. No one can truly predict the future, but I think the signs of some things to come are clear.

Hybrid workforces will be the norm. It won't be potentially embarrassing to tell people that your business doesn't have a central office and that you work from home. In fact, you will be treated with respect for being able to create and manage a modern workplace.

It won't be unusual to hear people say they work from home. It will no longer be viewed as a 'second-class citizen' kind of job.

Employees will make job choices based on the ability to work from home or remotely.

Workers will become more self-sufficient. When working remotely there will be no more asking an admin assistant to print or photocopy something for them, or – God forbid – to pick up their drycleaning.

Travelling for a one-hour meeting will become extremely unusual and the prevalence of video and telephone meetings will continue to rise.

Technology will continue to develop at an exponential rate to support these new ways of working. I can see the day where we all start appearing as holograms in offices around the world.[56]

Work will truly be a thing we do, not a place we go. Performance will focus strongly on outcomes achieved rather than hours spent sitting at a desk or computer.

We will finally see people being hired or trained specifically as 'managers', rather than management being a promotion for those people who are good at their job.

We will see a more worldwide spread of work. It's been coming for a long time with businesses offshoring parts of their business, or using the freelancer gig economy platforms like Upwork and Fiverr, but I believe we will start to see the traditional employee also being able to take advantage of the greater flexibility that comes with working in a distributed team. Rather than people moving out of regional areas to pursue careers in the capital cities, we will see a resurgence of people moving to those areas. Perhaps they are moving 'back home' to be closer to family and friends, or perhaps they are moving countries to explore a love of travel and experience while still being able to work for a company they love.

New homes will be designed to incorporate a home office as a standard inclusion.

Offices will be re-envisioned. The endless cubicles will fall away. We will see more spaces for meetings and collaborations and creativity. Maybe we will see the regions develop as more businesses create regional hubs.

---

56 I must say that I hope to see the day where we can say, 'Beam me up, Scotty'.

New jobs, focusing on the art of collaboration and connection (in physical and online ways) will be fuelled by the evolution of the workplace.

Hours of work will change to allow people to accommodate their personal circumstances and global time zones.

Eventually, governments around the world will catch up and change legislation to support the new ways of working while protecting employee rights. We will see the increased ability to make individual agreements around working hours, requirements for employers to pay allowances to minimum wage employees who are working from home and increased rights to request flexible arrangements like remote work.

## BE BRAVE

Take a deep breath. You've come a long way. Maybe you've mapped out a fully distributed team or a hybrid masterpiece, or maybe you are feeling overwhelmed with the work ahead. Keep your vision front and centre – not just in your mind, but in the minds of your team.

Become a great communicator and leader and bring your vision to reality. Take your business into the future of work.

Build your Homeforce.

# Useful resources

- If you want to create a digital vision board, try www.canva.com.
- Online mindmap tools:
  - www.miro.com
  - www.mindmeister.com.
- Organisational chart tools:
  - www.miro.com
  - www.lucidchart.com.
- Downloadable resources created by me that I have referred to during this book, which can be found at 3dhrlegal.com.au/homeforce/resources:
  - Job description template
  - Work from home self-assessment
  - Framework Homeforce Policy.
- Possible personality tests to research:
  - the Clifton Strengths test (my personal favourite)
  - The Hogan Assessments
  - Click colours
  - the Enneagram test
  - the Kolbe index.

- A quick Google search on 'how to work remotely' will turn up thousands of hits. Here are some recommended books:
  - *HBR Guide to Remote Work*, February 2021.
  - *Working from Home: Making the new normal work for you*, Karen Mangia, 2020.
  - *Work from Home Hacks: 500+ easy ways to get organised, stay productive, and maintain a work-life balance,* Aja Frost, December 2020.
  - *Working Remotely: Secrets to success for employees on distributed teams*, Teresa Douglas, Holly Gordon and Mike Webber, January 2020.
  - *The Tracksuit Economy: How to work productively and effectively from home*, Emma Heuston, 2018.
- As part of my research for this book, in addition to a survey and literature review, I conducted interviews with business leaders who have experience in working with and leading remote teams. Quotes from these interviews are scattered throughout the book. You can access the full-length interviews at 3dhrlegal.com.au/ homeforce/resources.

# Bibliography

'3 Tenets of a Strong Remote Culture', Nicholas C. Lovegrove, 22 December 2020, *Harvard Business Review* (hbr.org/2020/12/3-tenets-of-a-strong-remote-culture?autocomplete=true)

'5 Tips to Try Now As You Plan the Future of Your Workforce', Ashley Goldsmith, 11 May 2021, Fast Company (www.fastcompany.com/90635196/5-tips-to-try-now-as-you-plan-the-future-of-your-workforce?partner=rss&utm_source=rss&utm_medium=feed&utm_campaign=rss+fastcompany&utm_content=rss)

'9 Trends That Will Shape Work in 2021 and Beyond', Brian Kopp, 14 January 2021, *Harvard Business Review* (hbr.org/2021/01/9-trends-that-will-shape-work-in-2021-and-beyond?utm_medium=email&utm_source=newsletter_weekly&utm_campaign=insider_activesubs&utm_content=signinnudge&deliveryName=DM115785)

'A 2-Year Stanford Study Shows the Astonishing Productivity Boost of Working From Home', Scott Mautz, Inc, 2 April 2018 (www.inc.com/scott-mautz/a-2-year-stanford-study-shows-astonishing-productivity-boost-of-working-from-home.html)

'"A real shift": Women the big winners as work comes home', Bianca Hall and Royce Millar, *The Age*, (www.theage.com.au/politics/victoria/a-real-shift-women-the-big-winners-as-work-comes-home-20201030-p56a4b.html?_lrsc=76f3c6f9-d0cf-4f0e-9ba7-20c889d23c43)

'Adapting to the future of work', Richard Houston (www.linkedin.com/pulse/adapting-future-work-richard-houston/), 18 June 2021.

'An Evangelist for Remote Work Sees the Rest of the World Catch On', *The New York Times* (www.nytimes.com/2020/07/12/business/matt-mullenweg-automattic-corner-office.html)

'Behaviours of the World's Best Managers', Gallup, 30 December 2019, (www.gallup.com/workplace/272681/habits-world-best-managers. aspx?utm_source=workplace_newsletter&utm_medium=email&utm_ campaign=workplace_newsletter_dec_12292020&utm_content= doyourmanagers_textlink_3&elqTrackId=d5746e671bfb4026911d35b2c01 da577&elq=3354c170e31c45239507ccd205966fcb&elqaid=5655&elqat= 1&elqCampaignId=1183)

'Bosses and employees divided over working from home rules', *The Sydney Morning Herald*, 14 December 2020 (amp-smh-com-au.cdn.ampproject. org/c/s/amp.smh.com.au/business/workplace/bosses-and-employees-divided-over-working-from-home-rules-20201130-p56j3m.html)

'Building Australia's digital resilience – How technology strengthened business during COVID and beyond', Report by AlphaBeta Australia (3er1viui9wo30pkxh1v2nh4w-wpengine.netdna-ssl.com/wp-content/ uploads/prod/sites/583/2020/09/AlphaBeta-research.pdf)

'Characteristics of Employment, Australia', *ABS*, Catalogue No. 6333.0., August 2019,

'COVID-19s Impact on Culture', *AHRI*, August 2020 (www.ahri.com.au/ media/5024/ahri_augusthrculturereport_2020.pdf)

'Deloitte to Shut Four UK Offices as COVID-19 Entrenches Remote Working', Reuters, 18 October 2020, Money Control News (www.money control.com/news/world/deloitte-to-shut-four-uk-offices-as-covid-19-entrenches-remote-working-5976761.html)

*Demasi v Comcare (Compensation)* [2016] AATA 644 (26 August 2016).

'Give Your Remote Team Unstructured Time for Collaboration', Barbara Z Larson, 27 October 2020, *Harvard Business Review* (hbr.org/2020/ 10/give-your-remote-team-unstructured-time-for-collaboration?auto complete=true)

'Go Ahead, Tell Your Boss You Are Working From Home', Nicholas Bloom, TED Talk (www.youtube.com/watch?v=oiUyyZPIHyY&list=PLsRNoUx 8w3rMiDAN8WZilNFEWtqhsqh4D&index=8)

*HBR Guide to Remote Work*, Harvard Business Review Press, 2021

'How the Coronavirus Outbreak has – and hasn't – Changed the way Americans Work', Kim Parker, Juliana Menasce Horowitz and Rachel Minkin, Pew Research Center, 9 December 2020 (www.pewresearch.org/social-trends/2020/12/09/how-the-coronavirus-outbreak-has-and-hasnt-changed-the-way-americans-work/?=1)

'How to Build Trust and Boost Productivity Within Remote Teams', Gallup Article, 12 August 2020 (www.gallup.com/workplace/316931/build-trust-boost-productivity-within-remote-teams.aspx?utm_source=workplace_newsletter&utm_medium=email&utm_campaign=workplace_newsletter_dec_12292020&utm_content=engageremoteteams_textlink_2&elqTrackId=ba0af3d81b424d639b8794bc0b781568&elq=3354c170e31c45239507ccd205966fcb&elqaid=5655&elqat=1&elqCampaignId=1183)

'How to do Hybrid Right', Lynda Gratton, *Harvard Business Review* Magazine, May-June 2021 (hbr.org/2021/05/how-to-do-hybrid-right?utm_medium=email&utm_source=newsletter_weekly&utm_campaign=insider_activesubs&utm_content=signinnudge&deliveryName=DM129267&registration=success)

'How to Manage a Hybrid Team', Rebecca Knight, 7 October 2020, *Harvard Business Review* (hbr.org/2020/10/how-to-manage-a-hybrid-team?utm_medium=email&utm_source=newsletter_weekly&utm_campaign=insider_activesubs&utm_content=signinnudge&deliveryName=DM101488)

'How to Set Up a Remote Employee for Success on Day One', James M Citrin and Darleen DeRose, 10 May 2021, Harvard Business Review (hbr.org/2021/05/how-to-set-up-a-remote-employee-for-success-on-day-one?utm_medium=email&utm_source=newsletter_weekly&utm_campaign=insider_activesubs&utm_content=signinnudge&deliveryName=DM132438)

'HSBC Staff in Hong Kong can now Reportedly Work 4 Days a Week From Home: And they will get a $322 allowance to set up a home office', Grace Dean, 18 November 2020, Business Insider Australia (www.businessinsider.com.au/working-from-home-hsbc-hong-kong-remote-office-2020-11?r=US&IR=T)

'Informal Communication in an All-Remote Environment', GitLab, 2020, about.gitlab.com/company/culture/all-remote/informal-communication/)

'Investigating "Anywhere Working" as a Mechanism for Alleviating Traffic Congestion in Smart Cities', Hopkins, John L, & McKay, Judith (2019) *Technological Forecasting & Social Change* Vol 142, May pp258-272 (www. sciencedirect.com/science/article/abs/pii/S0040162518301549?via%3Dihub)

'Is Working from home good work of bad work? Evidence from Australian employees,' A.M. Dockery and Sherry Bawa, *Australian Journal of Labour Economics* Volume 17, Number 2, 2014, pp163-190.

'Key Working from Home Trends Emerging from COVID-19 – A Report to the Fair Work Commission', Dr John Hopkins and Professor Anne Bardoel, Swinburne University of Technology, November 2020 (www.fwc.gov.au/documents/sites/clerks-work-from-home/research/am202098-research-reference-list-su-241120.pdf)

'Microsoft's New 6-Word Remote Work Policy is Brilliant. Here's Why Your Company Should Steal It', Justin Bariso, Inc., 19 October 2020, (www.inc.com/justin-bariso/microsofts-new-6-word-remote-work-policy-is-brilliant-heres-why-your-company-should-steal-it.html)

No Office Required Podcast, Bruce Daisley

'NSW Remote Working Insights: Our experience during COVID-19 and what it means for the future of work', Council Research Paper, NSW Innovation and Productivity Council 2020.

'Performance Management Must Evolve to Survive COVID-19', Gallup article, 31 August 2020 (www.gallup.com/workplace/318029/performance-management-evolve-survive-covid.aspx?utm_source=workplace_newsletter &utm_medium=email&utm_campaign=workplace_newsletter_dec_ 12292020&utm_content=takemoreagile_textlink_4&elqTrackId=d81bae0 fb68f44c797db632cdffdafb3&elq=3354c170e31c45239507ccd205966fcb& elqaid=5655&elqat=1&elqCampaignId=1183)

'Personality Isn't Permanent', Benjamin Hardy PhD, 2020

'Preferences for Flexible Working Arrangements: Before, during and after COVID-19 – A Report to the Fair Work Commission', Professor Marian Baird AO and Daniel Dinale, University of Sydney, November 2020 (www.

fwc.gov.au/documents/documents/awardmod/variations/2020/am202098-research-report-bd-301120.pdf)

'Reimagining the Office and Work Life After COVID-19', by Brodie Boland, Aaron De Smet, Rob Palter and Aditya Sanghvi, 8 June 2020, McKinsey & Co, (www.mckinsey.com/business-functions/organization/our-insights/reimagining-the-office-and-work-life-after-covid-19)

'Remote Managers are Having Trust Issues', Sharon K. Parker, Caroline Knight, & Anita Keller, 30 July 2020, *Harvard Business Review* (hbr.org/2020/07/remote-managers-are-having-trust-issues)

'Remote Work Doesn't Have to Mean All-Day Video Calls', Marco Minervini, Darren Murph and Phanish Puranam, 9 September 2020, *Harvard Business Review* (hbr.org/2020/09/remote-work-doesnt-have-to-mean-all-day-video-calls?autocomplete=true)

'Successful Remote Teams Communicate in Bursts', Christopher Riedl and Anita Williams Woolley, 28 October 2020, *Harvard Business Review* (hbr.org/2020/10/successful-remote-teams-communicate-in-bursts?autocomplete=true)

'The Expectation Gap in the Future of Work', Boston Consulting Group, 14 December 2020 (www.bcg.com/en-au/publications/2020/understanding-the-expectation-gap-in-the-future-of-work-australia)

*The Five Dysfunctions of a Team* 2nd edition, Patrick Lencione. (2012)

'The Good, The Bad, and the Unknown About Telecommuting: Meta-analysis of individual consequences and mechanisms of distributed work', Academy of Management Best Conference Paper 2006 HR:D6 Authors: RAVI S. GAJENDRAN, DAVID A. HARRISON, Pennsylvania State University (journals.aom.org/doi/pdf/10.5465/ambpp.2006.27161834)

'The Implications of Working Without an Office', Ethan Bernstein, Hayley Blunden, Andrew Brodsky, Wonbin Sohn, and Ben Waber, *Harvard Business Review*, 15 July 2020 (hbr.org/2020/07/the-implications-of-working-without-an-office)

'The Remote Working Playbook: A guide for Newly Remote Individuals and Teams', Steve Glaveski

The Telework Kit, NSW RTA Teleworking Manual, May 2009 (www.voced. edu.au/content/ngv%3A59207)

'The Time to Negotiate an Annual Month of Remote Work May Be Now', Monica Buchanan Pitrelli, 10 May 2021 (www.cnbc.com/2021/05/10/ annual-workcation-tips-for-asking-for-a-month-of-remote-work.html)

'This Company's New 2-Sentence Remote Work Policy is the Best I've Ever Heard', Justin Bariso, Inc., 27 July 2020 (www.inc.com/justin-bariso/this-companys-new-2-sentence-remote-work-policy-is-best-ive-ever-heard.html)

'Three Character Traits Can Tell if Working From Home, or Working Remotely, Works For You', Rebecca Turner, 23 September 2019, ABC News (www.abc.net.au/news/2019-09-23/ three-traits-that-tell-if-you-are-suited-to-working-from-home/11531924)

'What Psychological Safety Looks Like in a Hybrid Workplace', Amy C Edmondson and Mark Mortensen, 19 April 2021, *Harvard Business Review* (hbr.org/2021/04/what-psychological-safety-looks-like-in-a-hybrid-workplace?utm_medium=email&utm_source=newsletter_weekly&utm_campaign=insider_activesubs&utm_content=signinnudge&deliveryName= DM129267)

'Work and Life in a Pandemic: An Update on Hours of Work and Unpaid Overtime Under COVID-19', Dan Nahum, The Centre for Future Work at the Australia Institute, November 2020 (d3n8a8pro7vhmx.cloudfront. net/theausinstitute/pages/3395/attachments/original/1605571432/ GHOTD_2020_formatted_FINAL_FOR_RELEASE.pdf?1605571432)

Work from Home Survey – Australia and New Zealand, HR Professional and HR Leader Feedback, ELMO (page.elmosoftware.com.au/rs/021-FIO-132/images/WFH%20Survey%20-%20HR%20Leader%20Report%20 FINAL%20210820.pdf?mkt_tok=eyJpIjoiTmpCcaE5USTVNbVF6WlR kbCIsInQiOiJvQ1ZOMGhcL0U3QlBKdzUzYmJWcHM4WE11bnl3 NExKeXpoU3JONFJsdDcyRGphld4Y29iSWF5OVwvTkdFYVprUjN6 XC82WVUyTlNkMzYyQUp4SEhXUXp2NTJ0ZTZtcK2ZmcE5pc2pa NzNFMWsyalNSTks0cndxVnF3FbnZKNUFIYXNydSJ9)

'Work Will Never Be The Same: Savvy business leaders are adapting to change that's already here', Bharat Khandelwal, Deborah Lovich, Joppe Bijlsma, Frank Breitling, Penny Metchev, Boston Consulting Group,

17 November 2020 (www.bcg.com/publications/2020/how-business-leaders-are-adapting-during-covid-19)

'Working Remotely: Careers, Management and Strategy', Gallup (www.gallup.com/workplace/316313/understanding-and-managing-remote-workers.aspx)

www.bcg.com/publications/2020/how-business-leaders-are-adapting-during-covid-19

www.cultureamp.com/blog/the-biggest-lie-in-hr-people-quit-managers/
www.mckinsey.com/business-functions/organization/our-insights/reimagining-the-postpandemic-workforce

www.ted.com/talks/robert_waldinger_what_makes_a_good_life_lessons_from_the_longest_study_on_happiness?language=en#t-116178

www.ted.com/talks/simon_sinek_how_great_leaders_inspire_action?language=en

# Acknowledgements

I'm a fortunate woman. I couldn't have produced this book, or do all of the things that I do, without my own incredible Homeforce. From my home life team to my work life team, I couldn't have done it without you all.

Thank you Evan, for giving me the space and quiet encouragement to pursue this goal of mine to become a published author. It made the world of difference knowing that you were there for the kids on all those times when I just needed to put my head down and write. Thanks for championing my dreams.

And to my beautiful children – Janika, Vesna and Zavier. You were the best little motivators ever. The joy on your faces each time you got to colour in a square on our chart because I had written another 1000 words was a huge energiser. (Although I know the motivator for all of you was the restaurant dinner we had planned to celebrate the finished draft!)

Lucy Dickens – I am forever grateful for our chance meeting and the deep friendship that came from it. Thank you for your encouragement, for doing a full edit of the first draft of this book when you knew I was super busy, for not complaining when I asked the same questions again and again, for inspiring me with your own achievements, and for always being willing to challenge my thinking with your thoughtful questions. That's what true friends do.

Clarissa Rayward, thank goodness you wrote a book! Who knows where I'd be now if I hadn't seen *Happy Lawyer, Happy Life* advertised in a Law Society email and found you at the end of the rainbow. Joining The Club and attending the inaugural Club Retreat (and every one since!) sparked so many amazing things in my life – The Juggle podcast, courses that I enrolled in, friendships I made with you and others in your community, and now, this book. Thank you for being an amazing friend and mentor.

Naomi Strelein, thank you my friend for being one of my earliest book editors. For asking me sense-checking questions, suggesting amendments and giving me such great encouragement.

Special thanks to my team at 3D HR Legal, especially Cara and Myra, for your support in bringing this book to life.

Andrew Griffiths, thank you for creating such a fantastic course with the framework and support I needed to help write this book – and the occasional (or not so occasional) motivating kick when that was needed too.

And thank you. Thank you for being the kind of leader who believes that remote/flexible work has benefits for organisations and individuals, who wants to implement a system which is set up for success not failure, and who is daring to take on the future of work head on.

# About Jo Alilovic

Jo Alilovic is the Director and founder of 3D HR Legal, an employment lawyer with 20 years' experience, author and flexible work advocate who leads by example.

Jo was an early adopter of the remote first and hybrid workforce, managing her own fully distributed team for the last five years. After over a decade working for the largest law firm in Western Australia, Jo's own business started as a bit of an accident – as so many good things do – when she decided to move down to Donnybrook with her family. At the time working remotely wasn't the done thing.

She quickly saw the opportunity to build a new style of law firm, one which would not only allow for location freedom and flexible work hours, but would also enable her to live out her dream to have both a successful career and a fulfilling family life. This desire also led to her co-founding 'The Juggle' podcast which in 2020 celebrated over 100 episodes and 68,000 downloads.

Her core values of fairness and flexibility are the foundation of her business and permeate her work. Her greatest love is teaching her clients how to improve their workplaces through education and training, whether one to one or in a group setting. Jo regularly speaks in professional circles and creates and delivers customised, engaging and actionable workplace training on issues such as flexible work practices, bullying, harassment and performance management.

Jo helps business owners create thriving workplace cultures by clearly articulating their minimum expectations, providing strategies to manage complaints and conflict and coaching leaders through difficult conversations. All of this means Jo's clients spend little time dealing with legal proceedings and more time focused on their business.

Jo lives in Perth, Western Australia with her husband and three children, and dog Dexter. If they aren't busy running between weekend sports events, you will often find them enjoying the quiet bush surroundings at their home in Donnybrook.

jo@3dhrlegal.com.au
www.3dhrlegal.com.au
www.linkedin.com/in/joanne-alilovic/

### Homeforce training for managers

Ready to educate and empower your managers to be successful in a hybrid or remote workplace?

Contact Jo to find out about her course for managers. Going beyond being a mere information session, the training is designed to provide insight into managing flexibility in a hybrid/remote workplace, and give your managers a framework to make flexibility successful for your whole team. Jo also offers ongoing one-on-one support for managers who need the 'just in time' coaching.

If you have a team of managers who are heading your remote workplace and would like to know more about this training, please email Jo at jo@3dhrlegal.com.au

### Homeforce consulting

Ready to apply what you've read here … ?

Jo works with a limited number of clients each quarter to help them implement the REMOTE framework in their business. Flexible and remote work practices have been given a significant boost since 2020, and they are here to stay. If you want to take advantage of the ongoing opportunities of these work practices, and be set up for the long term, then get in touch to see if you are a good fit to work with Jo and her team.

If you'd like to know more about working with Jo to implement the REMOTE framework, email her at jo@3dhrlegal.com.au

**Looking for an engaging speaker or customised training for your live or virtual event?**

Jo Alilovic is an experienced speaker and facilitator who inspires people to create workplaces we all want to work in. Her presentations are full of stories and practical tips that leave people with actionable ideas and the motivation to make them happen. She is able to draw as much on her employment law expertise and global research as her own personal experiences as a business owner and those of the clients she's been serving for the last 20 years.

Jo's favourite things to talk about include workplace flexibility, issues affecting women at work, the career/family juggle, bullying/harassment, and managing performance and difficult conversations.

*'Jo is a fantastic facilitator and trainer!*

*Jo's facilitation style was engaging and really connected with the audience. After sitting through back-to-back sessions, it was important to have facilitators with energy and passion to keep the audience engaged. Jo certainly did that. I would and will consider Jo to deliver similar training/education sessions within our business in the future.'*

Georgia Matters, People and Culture Project Specialist, Gold Road Resources

If you're interested in getting Jo to speak at your next event or customise training for your organisation, either face-to-face or virtually, please email jo@3dhrlegal.com.au

**Would you like to interview Jo Alilovic?**

Jo can speak with passion and authority about:

- The future of work
- Managing remote/hybrid teams
- Flexible work practices, and the benefits, challenges and how-to of making it work
- Being a small business owner
- Managing performance and conduct
- Preventing bullying and harassment at work
- The career/family juggle

If you would like to interview Jo about any of the above or her latest book *Homeforce: Building an engaged, connected home-based team*, please email jo@3dhrlegal.com.au